The
HALIGONIANS

*100 fascinating lives
from the Halifax region*

EDITED BY ROMA SENN

Formac Publishing Company Limited
Halifax

Formac Publishing Company Limited acknowledges the support of the Culture Division, Nova Scotia Department of Tourism, Culture and Heritage. We acknowledge the financial support of the Government of Canada through the Book Publishing Industry Development Program (BPIDP) for our publishing activities.

We acknowledge the support of the Canada Council for the Arts for our publishing program.

ONTARIO ARTS COUNCIL
CONSEIL DES ARTS DE L'ONTARIO

The Canada Council | Le Conseil des Arts
for the Arts | du Canada

Library and Archives Canada Cataloguing in Publication

The Haligonians : 100 fascinating lives from the Halifax region / edited by Roma Senn. Includes bibliographical references and index.

ISBN10: 0-88780-671-6
ISBN13: 978-0-88780-671-1

1. Halifax (N.S. : Regional municipality)—Biography.   2. Halifax (N.S. : Regional municipality)—History.   I. Senn, Roma, 1954-

FC2346.25.H34 2005   971.6'22'0099
C2005-904524-8

Formac Publishing Company Limited
5502 Atlantic Street
Halifax, Nova Scotia B3H 1G4
www.formac.ca

Printed and bound in China

Visual Credits

Alderney Gate Public Library: p.62; Art Gallery of Nova Scotia: p.66, *Halifax's Northwest Arm*, Formac, 2003; p.91 (Lewis Smith), *The Artists' Halifax: Portraits of the Town and Harbour through 250 Years*, Formac, 2003; p.104 (John O'Brien), *The Artists' Halifax: Portraits of the Town and Harbour through 250 Years*, Formac, 2003; Julian Beveridge: p.136, *Titanic Remembered: The Unsinkable Ship and Halifax*, Formac, 2001; Black Cultural Centre for Nova Scotia: p.25; p.43, *Halifax: The First 250 Years*, Formac, 1999; p.106; p.111, *Halifax: The First 250 Years*, Formac, 1999; p.116 (Rosemary Eaton); Cole Harbour Rural Heritage Society: p.120 (Rosemary Eaton); Dalhousie Art Gallery: p.95, *Halifax: The First 250 Years*, Formac, 1999; Dance Nova Scotia: p.19; Dartmouth Heritage Museum: cover; p.1; P. Delefes: p.77, *Peoples of the Maritimes: Greeks*, Four East Publications, 2000; Fort Sackville Foundation: p.13; p.83; p.118 (Anneke Betlam); Gary Castle Photography: p.27, *Heritage Houses of Nova Scotia*, Formac, 2003; p.29; George Georgakakos: p.40; Halifax Regional Fire and Emergency: p.130; Maritime Command Museum: p.100, *Halifax: The First 250 Years*, Formac, 1999; Nova Scotia Archives and Records Management: p.7 (W. Chase); p.23, *Halifax: The First 250 Years*, Formac, 1999; p.34 (Albert G. Hoit); p.46, *Halifax's Northwest Arm*, Formac, 2003; p.58 (Nova Scotia Portraits, Cunard); p.64 (Notman Studios); p.67, *Halifax Street Names*, Formac, 2002; p.70 (Notman Studios); p.81 (Abbie Lane Photo Albums); p.87 (R.V. Harris Collection); p.94 (Notman Studios); p.124, *Halifax Street Names*, Formac, 2002; p.131, *Halifax: The First 250 Years*, Formac, 1999; p.135 (Notman Studios), *Titanic Remembered: The Unsinkable Ship and Halifax*, Formac, 2001; Nova Scotia Museum: p.3, *Halifax's Northwest Arm*, Formac, 2003; Nova Scotia Sport Hall of Fame: p.51; p.54; p.93; Oland Brewery: p.105; Pier 21: p.53; Private Collections: p.10; p.11; p.15; p.24; p.28, p.35; p.38; p.41; p.44; p.48; p.50; p.69; p.75; p.79, *Titanic Remembered: The Unsinkable Ship and Halifax*, Formac, 2001; p.80; p.82; p.85; p.103; p.108; p.112; p.127; Rockingham Heritage Society: p.60; Keith Vaughan: p.37, *Nova Scotia Colourguide (6th Edition)*.

CONTENTS

DEDICATION

In loving memory of my father

Dilip Kumar Senn
1921-2001

INTRODUCTION

Behind Halifax's familiar history hides a treasure trove of stories about remarkable people who shaped their communities in many different ways. Through the generosity of our storytellers — local historians and writers who work at keeping collective memories alive — we have compiled this collection of more than 100 fascinating men and women and their tales of achievement, heroism, tragedy and pathos.

The profiles in this book are presented in alphabetical sequence, with the contributor's name following the essay. Readers can find information about the contributors at the end of the book.

All of the people profiled in this book spent some part of their lives in Halifax or its surrounding communities, including Dartmouth, Cole Harbour, Bedford and Sambro. Their stories span the city's history, since its settlement in 1749, and one of the criteria for selection was that each person must be buried or have a memorial to them in the area. The years of birth and death are given and, in most cases, a record of where they are buried, as well.

In choosing stories that fell between the cracks of history, we made sure to include women who left their mark by defying the social stereotypes of their time. We also tried to present an inclusive history that brings out once-silenced voices from Halifax's Mi'kmaq and black communities.

In addition to featuring volunteers who tirelessly helped immigrants as they disembarked from the transatlantic crossing, the selection of profiles in this book includes leaders of various ethnic communities, revealing the multicultural character of Halifax. There are also profiles of men and women who have contributed significantly to the arts in the Halifax area.

Thanks are due to the more than 60 contributors, and special thanks are offered to Ann MacVicar, chair of the Fort Sackville Foundation, who graciously agreed to co-ordinate writers and stories from the Bedford area. In addition, there are those people who generously offered time and expertise, especially Pat and Jim Lotz, Roxanne Rees, Gus Wedderburn and the knowledgeable archivists at Nova Scotia Archives and Records Management — Lois Yorke, Philip Hartling and Garry Shutlak. The reference librarians at the Spring Garden Road Memorial Public Library patiently looked up dozens of obituaries, and the Halifax Regional Municipality opened up the Old Burying Grounds for me in late November.

Thanks are also due to Allan Doyle, Nova Scotia Tourism and Culture, Henry Bishop of the Black Cultural Centre for Nova Scotia, Anita Price at the Dartmouth Heritage Museum, Stephen Coutts at the Nova Scotia Sport Hall of Fame, Carrie-Ann Smith at Pier 21, Chris Mills of the Nova Scotia Lighthouse Preservation Society and Marilyn Gurney at the Maritime Command Museum. Elizabeth Eve, the senior editor at Formac Publishing, offered good advice and encouragement. Lastly, I'd like to thank my family, Greg, Bridget and Christopher Arsenault, who helped along the way.

Roma Senn
Halifax, N.S.
July 2005

William Ancient presides over the burial service of victims of the wreck of the SS Atlantic *at Lower Prospect, N.S., April 1873.*

WILLIAM J. ANCIENT
1836-1908
Buried at St. John's Cemetery, Halifax

In the spring of 1873, one of the most spectacular North Atlantic marine disasters of the late nineteenth century brought fleeting worldwide attention to Halifax. Before dawn on April Fool's Day, the White Star luxury liner SS *Atlantic* grounded on Mars Rock, off Meaghers (Mosher) Island, 1.6 kilometres from Terence Bay. Bound from Liverpool, England, to New York with 976 on board, the vessel had encountered heavy weather and was detouring into Halifax. Faulty navigation, however, led it onto the rocks instead.

Within 10 minutes the SS *Atlantic* broke up and began to sink. Crewmembers secured a line to land and in the darkness some 250 people were brought ashore in the darkness. Fishermen from Lower Prospect arrived at dawn with three small boats and saved another 150. A second rescue party from Terence Bay brought the resident Church of England clergyman, William Johnson Ancient.

Ancient had been an able seaman in the Royal Navy during the Crimean War before coming to Halifax, where he read scripture at the dockyard. In 1867, he was sent to Terence Bay, a "destitute and desolate" fishing community some 24 kilometres outside the city. His background fitted him well for his new flock who were, according to him, frequently "a little disordered especially in connection with Rum [and] think it hard that they cannot drink, fiddle and dance yet be considered good church members."

By early afternoon on April 1, 1873, only two people remained alive on the SS *Atlantic*: the first officer, John W. Firth, and a boy named John Hindley — both lashed to the mizzen-mast rigging. The wreck was listing at a 50-degree angle and the seas were rough, but as Ancient later recounted in sworn evidence, the fishermen [were] walking about the shore in search of such articles as might be thrown on shore, and not making the least efforts to rescue them." When the clergyman asked to be rowed out, the wreckers hesitated, suggesting this would certainly be his death.

As they approached, Hindley fell from the rigging and was plucked from the roaring waters. Ancient scrambled aboard, passed a line to Firth, and instructed him to "put your confidence in me and the Lord and move when I tell you." As they struggled, a huge sea swept Firth overboard, and in horror he cried out: "O Lord I have broken my shins." Ancient roared: "Never mind your shins, man! It is your life we are after."

The international press seized upon the story of the SS *Atlantic* with a zeal surpassed only when the *Titanic* sank nearly 40 years later. Ancient was lionized for his achievement, which was merely the climax of courageous efforts from a community of seafarers. The press created a stalwart Victorian hero "six feet in height and strongly built [with] a genial face, a bright eye, a clear head and a warm heart."

Over 500 people perished in the wreck of the SS *Atlantic*. Those who survived remembered forever the cries of the women passengers as they floated off into the darkness and death, weighted down by their voluminous clothing.

— *Lois Yorke*

MARIA L. ANGWIN
1849-1898
Buried at the Dartmouth Public Cemetery

Although women doctors are an accepted and integral part of health-care delivery today, the situation was very different 120 years ago in Halifax. It was an age when gender bias decreed that only men were capable of providing professional medical care

In September 1884, Maria Louisa Angwin became the first woman licensed to practise medicine in Nova Scotia. Several other ambitious young women had preceded her to the United States for training, but none had dared return; she was the first, perhaps the most determined, and her credentials were impeccable.

An 1882 graduate from Woman's Medical College, New York Infirmary for Women and Children, Angwin interned at Boston's New England

Hospital for Women and Children and then took post-graduate training in London, England. The Provincial Medical Board could neither ignore her qualifications nor refuse her application to practise.

Beginning in 1882, Dr. Angwin lived and worked in downtown Halifax for 14 years, providing medical services primarily to underprivileged women and children. As the city's first female physician, and one with a strong social conscience, she inevitably attracted attention. Arguably, she was Halifax's first "new woman" — that faintly ambivalent 1890s term used to describe independent and progressive females. Known for her short hair and determined stand against alcohol and cigarettes, Dr. Angwin was advanced in her thinking, broad-minded and eccentric. She was an early telephone subscriber, and patients ringing her doorbell were routinely greeted by a resident parrot announcing, "Someone wants the doctor." A contemporary remembered her as "a woman of courage ready for any emergency, versatile, afraid of nothing, answering all calls to any section of the city by day or night" — armed, as she herself said, with only a hat-pin.

In New York City, she had trained under the famous Blackwell sisters, Drs. Emily and Elizabeth, and absorbed their advocacy of preventive medicine and educating the young, particularly females, in moral and physical hygiene — in other words, community-centred social services and family planning. In an age when women could not vote and were routinely excluded from higher education, Angwin championed female suffrage, supported entitlement to education, lectured on hygiene, and spoke out against systemic barriers raised against women entering the workforce. Such ideas were no longer new to late-19th-century Halifax, but they were still controversial. In general, the community regarded Angwin with curiosity, suspicion and more than a little distrust. Respectable middle-class women avoided her and continued to patronize the male medical establishment; but the poor and disadvantaged welcomed her, especially for her skills in obstetrics and pediatrics.

In April 1898, Angwin fell ill while travelling in the United States, died suddenly and was brought home for burial. Local newspapers described the "dull and dogged opposition which pioneers always encounter," but concluded that "faithful, attentive, conscientious, she laboured in her profession far beyond her strength, while her womanly sympathy and medical knowledge won the friendship as well as the trust of her patients." Even the *Maritime Medical News* grudgingly acknowledged that she was "greatly respected, not only in her duties as a physician, but also in every work that tended to elevate fallen humanity."

— *Lois Yorke*

EDWARD FRANCES ARAB
1915-1944
Buried at the Canadian War Dead Cemetery at Bergen Ob Zoom, Netherlands

In 1937, Edward Arab was one of the youngest students to graduate from Dalhousie University's Law School.

Edward Frances Arab excelled in everything he attempted. Eddy, as he is still fondly known, was the grandson of Abraham and Annie Arab, and the son of Louis and Sadie (Assaf) Arab. His grandfather was the first person from Diman, North Lebanon, to come to Nova Scotia.

Eddy graduated from Dalhousie Law School in 1937 at the age of 22, one of the youngest to graduate in law from that noted institution. He was a top student and an athlete, winning trophies in soccer, swimming and boxing. He and a fellow student, John Fisher, made up an unbeatable debating team that travelled to debating tournaments throughout the Maritime provinces. They were never defeated.

After graduating with honours, Eddy articled with a well-known law firm called J. E. Rutledge. He was invited to join the firm but decided to open his own practice. His work was mostly in criminal law, and he gained a reputation for working on cases that helped defeat prejudice and racism. Throughout his career he gave instructions that no Lebanese, black or poor person should be turned away, regardless of whether they could pay, which many could not.

Eddy counted friends from all nationalities, races and religions. Proud of his Lebanese heritage, he was a founding member and the first president of the Canadian Lebanon Society, which was established in 1938.

Eddy enlisted for the war in the spring of 1941. He could have stayed close to home but chose to serve overseas: "I did not join this man's army to sit on my butt in Aldershot, I am going to fight for my Country."

After joining the army, he was home on furlough, spending an evening at the well-known Greek Club run by George Monopoulous, a friend and a client. A big, fierce fellow called Eaton was causing a disturbance and attacked Eddy with racist remarks. Eddy, who wasn't a big man, said calmly: "Well, I guess this should be settled once and for all. Why don't we go behind the club to the plant wharf [a loading dock near the club]?" Eddy headed for the door. When he looked back, Eaton had sat down and apparently ceased his notorious attacks for good.

When the Allied Forces were pushing into Holland Eddy was a lieutenant in the Lincoln and Welland Regiment. He was leading his regiment when they came under extremely heavy enemy fire. He was wounded and fell back. After the medics attended his wounds, he forged ahead a second time with his troops — an act that inevitably led to his death.

Lieutenant Edward Francis Arab was killed with most of his platoon on the border of Belgium and Holland in 1944 at the age of 29. He is buried outside Amsterdam in the Canadian War Dead Cemetery at Bergen Ob Zoom.

— Patricia Arab

SOPHIE (GULESSARIAN) ARAKELIAN
1903-1966
Ashes buried at Camp Hill Cemetery, Halifax

Sophie Gulessarian, a Christian Armenian, was nine when the Turks forced her family out of their home in Aintab, Armenia. Her parents and four siblings trudged around the desert, living in a tent. After her father died in 1914, the family was sent to a concentration camp as part of what Canada has called genocide; between 1915 and 1923, the Turks killed 1.5 million Armenians.

Soon after Sophie's mother gave birth, the Turks seized the baby boy and

Sophie Arakelian (right) and friend Katie Tzakarakis, c. 1934.

the family never saw him again. Her mother disappeared, and her two younger brothers and a sister died from starvation. Sophie and her sister Zaroohi survived because they embroidered beautifully, and for this they received one bun and water each day.

Sophie eventually went to work as a house girl for a Moslem family, not knowing her sister's whereabouts. When the war ended, she was sent to an orphanage in Damascus, Syria, and found Zaroohi. She attended school at the orphanage and, when it closed, she lived in another one in Beirut, Lebanon. There, she learned to speak English and saw a photograph of a man in Canada looking for an Armenian wife.

In 1922, Sophie and a friend set off for Canada to meet the man she would marry. They travelled to Marseilles, by train to Paris, and then sailed across the English Channel to Liverpool. While waiting for the boat to take her to Canada, Sophie, adventurous and smart, decided to see Liverpool. She picked up a rock and marked Xs on the ground to find her way back to the docks.

Sophie sailed across the Atlantic Ocean on the *Konopik*, arriving in Halifax in April 1922. There, she met Sarkis Arakelian. On the same day, an Anglican minister married the couple, with Armenian–Nova Scotians standing as witnesses.

Sarkis ran the Marathon Restaurant on Duke Street and operated the Empire Photo Studio on Barrington Street. One day Sophie watched Sarkis take pictures and said it looked easy. After she took an acceptable picture, Sarkis told her she could work in the studio herself.

Sarkis died at 53, leaving Sophie, 39, with a young family. While raising her six children, she continued to run the studio and remained active at All Saints Cathedral by participating in the Mother's Union, a fund-raising group for the church and its members.

Her family has fond memories of singing hymns together and Sophie's wonderful Armenian cooking.

— *Sophie Langille-Broderick*

BERTHA OGILVIE ARCHIBALD

1889-1984
Buried at Brookside Cemetery, Bedford

Bertha Archibald was the first female pharmacist to study and receive a diploma in pharmacy at Dalhousie University.

She had just started work at the Victoria General Hospital when the

Halifax Explosion occurred. After the awful noise and crashing windows, she ducked to safety behind a counter. Following the explosion, her superiors helped the injured and she managed the dispensary alone. "I never worked so hard in all my life," she told the *Chronicle-Herald*. "I think that God gave me strength."

Bertha Archibald, c.1955.

Born in Bedford in 1899, Archibald was the daughter of Joseph and Amelia, and one of five children. She took an early interest in nursing and while she was in Calgary awaiting an opening in a training program, an outbreak of para-typhoid fever gave her the chance to begin nursing.

A visit to the hospital pharmacy fascinated her and, with the encouragement of a female pharmacist, Archibald returned to Nova Scotia to study pharmacy. She attended the Nova Scotia Technical College and then spent three years at a Bedford pharmacy before attending Dalhousie University for a year. Her diploma is displayed today in the Pharmacy College at Dalhousie.

Archibald served as head pharmacist at the Victoria General Hospital for nearly 30 years, commuting daily by train from her Bedford home. Once, when the train was delayed because of snow, she walked 16 kilometres to work, admitting in a 1977 interview that she'd cheated a bit: "I caught a street car when I got to Halifax."

Archibald was also a poet and writer, contributing to a variety of professional and general interest publications. "A poet with the gift of song. She sings well and has something to say," noted a headline in the *Chronicle-Herald* in 1958.

An ardent practising Christian, she attended the Bedford Baptist Church where her parents had been founding members in 1899. Archibald served as a Sunday school teacher and proudly watched as her entire class of 10 were baptized in Bedford Basin and received as church members.

When Archibald retired in 1946, one year after the end of World War II, she spent many years in active retirement at Victoria Hall, living until she was 95.

— *C. Nelson Kennedy*

EDITH JESSIE ARCHIBALD
1854-1936
Buried at Camp Hill Cemetery, Halifax

Edith Jessie Archibald was one of a handful of "feminist superstars" in Halifax who worked tirelessly for women's suffrage until the vote was won at the federal and provincial levels in 1918.

The daughter of a Nova Scotia-born British diplomat, Edith married her second cousin Charles Archibald in June 1874; they had four children. For the next 18 years, Charles managed the Gowrie Colliery in Port Morien, Cape Breton. In Cow Bay, Edith became active in the Women's Christian Temperance Union (WCTU), and she assumed leadership roles at the local, regional, provincial and national levels of the organization. Her lengthy president's reports suggest that she must have been an engaging and powerful orator. She drew effectively on evangelical rhetoric to rally the enthusiasm and support of members, especially for the right to vote:

> Come out with me on the watch tower, O discouraged
> sisters! and, as you look over the battle-field of the world,
> see how the blood-stained banners of the Cross are ever
> increasingly victorious over the hosts of sin and darkness!

In 1894, the Archibalds moved to Halifax where Edith continued her suffrage and reform work. She was among the founders of the Victorian Order of Nurses in Halifax, and an active member of the Halifax Ladies Musical Club, which promoted opportunities for women in performing, composing and teaching music.

During the war Edith, like many of her associates on the LCW, became active in war work through the Red Cross. She was put in charge of the provincial Red Cross Department for the relief of prisoners of war, a suitable job for the daughter of a diplomat. The task was not completed until 1919 when the last of the prisoners returned to Canada.

After the war Edith continued to actively support philanthropic and cultural work in Halifax, remaining active in the Royal Nova Scotia Historical Society, the Halifax Ladies Musical Club and the children's hospital. She was also the "fairy godmother" of Rainbow Haven, a camp for poor children.

When not engaged in good works, she spent her time writing. She published a biography of her father, *Life and Letters of Sir Edward Mortimer Archibald*, a history of the Red Cross during the war, and *The Token*, first produced as a play in 1924 and later published in 1927.

Her death in May 1936 was front-page news in all five Halifax newspapers. The *Halifax Chronicle* claimed she was one of the most outstanding women in the provinces. More recently she has been commemorated for her contribution to the Canadian suffrage movement by the Historical Sites and Monuments Board with a plaque in her honour at the Local Council of Women house at the corner of South Park and Inglis Streets.

—Janet Guildford

GLADYS BEAVER
1889-1965
Buried at St. James Anglican Church Cemetery, Port Dufferin

On Christmas morning 1965, Gladys Beaver of West Quoddy died in the Eastern Shore Memorial Hospital. Her obituary noted that she had been active in school, church and community-related activities including the Red Cross. Her obituary, however, neglected to mention her business initiative, which marked a milestone for transportation along the Eastern Shore in 1919.

Gladys Beaver, daughter of Robert and Mary Ellen Jewers, was born in Ecum Secum but spent most of her life in West Quoddy. She was a stenographer for J.S. Hubley & Co. (groceries, provisions and insurance, Agricola Street, Halifax) for several years prior to her marriage to Merle F. Ettinger in 1913. Two years later, Merle died in Halifax.

Gladys Beaver, c.1910.

The *Truro Daily News*, August 8, 1919, announced that Mary Ellen Jewers and Gladys Ettinger had recently established the Quoddy-Halifax Motor Car Express. They also had "a neat and roomy garage, immediately opposite the well kept general store, so ably and efficiently conducted by Mrs. G.P. Ettinger." Ewart Beaver, who had been wounded at Vimy Ridge in World War I, drove the Ford passenger express, leaving Quoddy on Tuesday and Thursday and returning from the Dartmouth Ferry Wharf on Wednesday and Friday. Gladys married Ewart Beaver in September 1919.

The newspaper also noted that "the road is very bad in places, a disgrace to Halifax M.P.P.s, yet this staunch Ford travels with wonderful ease and good speed." Nevertheless, the 148-kilometre one-way trip took eight hours. Gladys Beaver constantly repaired or replaced the isinglass side windows, damaged by alders that grew beside Number 7 Highway. The taxi was occasionally stuck in quagmire-like mud holes in springtime. It was pulled out by oxen.

The taxi service was mentioned in one verse of an untitled ballad by an anonymous composer. It told of a man who invited the village schoolteacher to a concert and dance in the 1920s or 1930s:

> Went out in the street, hailed a taxi
> Ewart Beaver said "Where shall we go?"
> I said in a dignified manner
> "Take us to Port Dufferin Hall."

The Quoddy-Halifax Motor Car Express, later renamed Beaver Taxi, operated until approximately 1935.

— *Philip Hartling*

JAMES KOVAL (J.K.) BELL
1908-1994
Buried in Saint John, New Brunswick

J. K. Bell, the founder of the Marine Workers' Federation and one of the finest trade unionists of his time, worked tirelessly throughout his life for workers, their families and anyone else in need.

Born in Halifax in 1908, Bell, who was known by everyone as J. K., spent his early life travelling the country trying to find a job. After World War I broke out, he finally settled in New Brunswick to work at the Saint John Drydock. This is where he joined the union movement, eventually founding the Marine Workers' Union.

J. K. was a left-leaning social activist, but most people considered him a communist although he was always quick to point out that he had never joined the communist party. He used to say with a grin: "I read the local socialist paper, and I am called a communist, yet I read the *Financial Post* and no one calls me a capitalist."

When the Nova Scotia Federation of Labour was established in 1956, its constitution banned "any organization controlled by a non-democratic element" including individuals "espousing communism, fascism or other totalitarianism." J. K. was the sole speaker to oppose this motion: "It takes all types of people to make up a local union," he told the *Chronicle-Herald*. "But in passing this passage you are endangering the autonomy of affiliated organizations." He cast the only "nay" vote.

In the early sixties, J. K. actively supported the community co-operative movement, founding the Capital Credit Union, a funeral co-op and a housing co-op. These efforts aimed at providing affordable necessities for working people and their families. J. K. realized early in his trade union life that, although a union protected workers' rights in their workplace, the needs of workers and their families transcended the workplace. He knew as well that workers' rights in a collective agreement could be taken away by government, and he lobbied all government levels on issues important to workers and their families for dignity and justice for all.

His sister, Mary, remembers their mother buying them new winter coats when they were young. All the children, including J. K., wore their new coats to school the next day. When they returned home, J. K. was missing his new coat. His mother, upset about the coat, asked about it. With some prodding, he said he had given his coat to a poor coat-less boy. "Jimmy, we're poor," she said. "I have my summer coat," he replied, which he wore for the rest of the winter.

J. K. addressed everyone as "ole boy." In fact, he is the subject of Sue Calhoun's book *Ole Boy: Memories of a Canadian Labour Leader J.K. Bell.*

— *Les Holloway*

WILLIAM BOWIE
1782-1819
Buried in the Old Burying Grounds, Halifax

William Bowie was one of the last men in Nova Scotia to be killed in a duel. A popular and respected member of Halifax society, his death shocked the community.

Bowie came to Halifax from Inverness, Scotland, in 1803 and became a successful merchant for Bowie and DeBlois, a firm that made a fortune selling the cargo privateers looted at sea.

During a Supreme Court trial, Richard Uniacke Jr., a lawyer and the son of the then attorney-general, addressed the jury and made comments that Bowie found offensive, perhaps accusing him of being a smuggler.

Bowie challenged Uniacke to a duel, which was illegal in Nova Scotia at the time. They fought between four and five in the morning near Lady Hammond Road in a grove of the governor's farm. The duellists took their 12 paces, turned and fired their pistols. No one was injured during the first round. It has been suggested that Uniacke's second, Edward M'Swiney, "a fire-eating Irishman," insisted on a second round. Bowie was hit in the chest, with a bullet lodged in his right side. He was carried to a nearby farm and died later that July day. At his well-attended funeral, the flags flew at half-mast on the ships in Halifax Harbour. Bowie was 37. His friends erected his gravestone in the Old Burying Grounds with this inscription: "Strict integrity and a high sense of honour rendered him respected as a merchant. A warm benevolent sound disposition made him beloved as a man."

Uniacke and M'Swiney were charged with murder; Stephen DeBlois, Bowie's second, was charged with a misdemeanour. "(T)he greatest show trial in Nova Scotia history" took place within a week, although Dean Jobb in *Shades of Justice* says the outcome was never really in doubt. No one would convict a well-connected gentleman. Uniacke went on to become a judge of the Supreme Court. He died at the age of 45, some saying the duel had shortened his life.

— *Roma Senn*

GUNTER BUCHTA
1924-1997
Cremated in Halifax

As Canadian households scrambled to purchase their first television sets in the mid-1950s, the CBC unveiled a musical variety program out of Halifax called Don Messer's Jubilee. This program regularly featured a group of dancers called "Buchta" and they captured the imaginations of young and old alike.

The dance group was the brainchild of Gunter Buchta, a German ex-soldier who had suffered a leg wound behind the Russian Front during World War II. "The doctor said I would die if they didn't amputate and I said: 'You are not taking my leg.'" An operation followed and his leg was saved. Another doctor told him to try dancing as a kind of therapy. The young sol-

Gunter Buchta poses with students Jane Edgett (left) and Pauline Alberts at a leadership training session hosted by Dance Nova Scotia in the late 1970s. Edgett's current position on the world panel of judges for international Dance Sport is evidence of Buchta's legacy.

dier, who had studied law, soon discovered he had a natural talent for dance and, following the war, he and his young wife Irma immigrated to Halifax.

As they danced and struggled with English in their new country, someone from the Maritime Conservatory of Music approached them about starting a dance department there. Buchta taught the European style of ballroom dancing, toured public schools and gave demonstrations. He became a founding member of the Atlantic Branch of the Canadian Dance Teachers Association (CDTA) and attained his international teaching accreditation in England. The standard of dance grew at the Conservatory until the Buchta

Dancers were born. Through the power of television, Buchta introduced highland, tap and folk dancing to the program's expanding repertoire.

Dance Nova Scotia (DANS) was founded in 1974 and Buchta was its first executive director. It was an organization that promoted every form of dance at both amateur and professional levels throughout the province. Buchta not only taught, he was also a well-known international judge of dance and travelled extensively in the United States and Europe. His contribution to dance was recognized when he became a Life Member of the Imperial Society of Teachers of Dancing. He also received an award from the International Dance Teachers Association in Blackpool, England.

A sophisticated gentleman, Buchta was often seen walking down Spring Garden Road on his way to the DANS office, impeccably groomed in his dark coat and white scarf, his thick hair immaculate, with an imperceptible limp. When asked why he stayed in Nova Scotia instead of going to Toronto or Montreal, he would smile and state simply: "We did well here."

— *Pam Lutz*

KATE CARMICHAEL
1950-2001

When Kate Carmichael was told she was dying of leukemia, she didn't quit her job or take off for an exotic destination. She had too much to do. A long-time champion in the effort to revitalize Halifax's downtown core, Carmichael continued to inspire those around her to the end, working "harder, faster and smarter" between blood transfusions — sometimes in spite of great pain — to do as much as she could in the three months doctors said she had left.

Carmichael, who was born in England in 1950, immigrated to Ontario with her family at age 7 and to Halifax at age 12. She married in 1972 and discovered her passion for community involvement as a young mother in Lunenburg. There she became chair of the Parent Teacher Association, a member of the School Board in 1988 and eventually Chair of the Board in 1990. Later that year, she returned to Halifax and became involved in politics. She won a place in Halifax City Council for Ward 2, Halifax South End, only to lose her seat a year later in the amalgamation election of 1995. It was after this that Carmichael was approached to head up the Downtown Halifax Business Commission, which would become the focus, and the source, of her energy for the remainder of her life.

Carmichael credited her passion for her work and the inspiration she derived from each small victory she achieved, to her survival —

nine months past the time she was originally given by doctors. Carmichael said she was like anyone confronted suddenly with death: afraid to die.

In spite of both fear and frustration, she continued to give in every way she could. Already a well-known figure in Halifax, Carmichael spoke openly with the national media of her disease and of dying, giving comfort and hope to those attempting to come to grips with similar situations. Her continued determination to improve the downtown area in spite of her illness acted as a catalyst to get necessary meetings scheduled, actions taken and balls rolling.

Spunky to the very end, Carmichael resisted suggestions from friends and family that she stay at home and relax. "That's not what I'm about," she said. "This is what makes me alive." The city of Halifax could not have hoped for a better champion and named a downtown street in her honour. To carry on Carmichael's legacy, a series of talks called "The Carmichael Lectures" are held each year in her memory, continuing efforts to rejuvenate Halifax's downtown core.

— *Lindsay O'Reilly*

PETER CARTCEL
HANGED IN 1749 IN HALIFAX
Likely buried in the Old Burying Grounds, Halifax

Peter Cartcel was the first person in Halifax to face a murder trial after the founding of the town. A French settler who spoke little English, Cartcel arrived at the same time as Governor Edward Cornwallis at a place that consisted of a few wharves and fewer buildings. It is surprising Cartcel was here at all, given that France and England were enemies. "Cartcel stood out like a sore thumb among the settlers, soldiers and sailors who had braved the voyage from England in the summer of 1749," wrote Dean Jobb in *Bluenose Justice: True Tales of Mischief, Mayhem and Murder*.

On August 26, 1749, Cartcel, a crewmember on the *Baltimore*, exchanged angry words with Abraham Goodsides, a boatswain's mate on the *Beaufort*. Later that day, the two men met again on the *Beaufort* with Goodsides asking Cartcel why he "used him ill" and "if he would fight him." With his open hand, Goodsides slapped Cartcel across the face. According to witnesses on the ship, Cartcel responded by shoving a 10-centimetre knife, valued at two pence, deep into Goodsides's chest. Goodsides immediately fell to the floor crying out "I am gone." Before he could be subdued, Cartcel wounded two other men.

Halifax had no court system and no one trained in law. However, five days after the murder, the General Court convened *The King vs. Cartcel* at a waterfront warehouse, the first murder case to be tried under English law in what would become Canada.

Cartcel, who pleaded not guilty, asked the Council of Twelve for an interpreter. Several witnesses were called for the prosecution and Goodsides's mates on the *Beaufort* related similar stories about the incident. Constable Roger Snowden told the court about the earlier exchange of words. Cartcel did not have anyone to represent him and declined to call any witnesses. A half-hour after the testimony was delivered, the jury returned with a guilty plea. Cartcel was executed within a week of the murder.

Nearly two centuries later, Joseph Chisholm, a Nova Scotia chief justice and an amateur historian, examined the Cartcel case and found it wanting, although Cornwallis's superiors in England lauded the swift execution of justice. A jury, properly instructed on the distinction between murder and manslaughter, would have found that the homicide was committed in the heat of passion and would perhaps have delivered a different verdict. The Honourable Chief Justice Chisholm said: "One cannot help feeling that it fell far short of ideal justice."

— *Roma Senn*

ROBERT CHAMBERS
1903-1996
Buried at Fairview Cemetery, Halifax

Robert Chambers, who was born in Wolfville in 1903, left Nova Scotia as a young man to pursue a career as an illustrator in New York City. He worked on an edition of *Aesop's Fables* and picked up extra money designing the covers of pulp novels and tabloid magazines.

Returning to Halifax in the '30s, Chambers took a job with the *Halifax Herald* as a cartoonist and illustrator. What followed was a forty-year career at the drafting table for which he was lauded by politicians and victims, and much loved by newspaper readers.

Chambers was best known for his genial lampooning of Nova Scotian, Canadian, and World leaders. In an age of political cynicism or realism (depending on your view), Chambers' work hearkened back to a spirited distrust (as opposed to disgust) of politicians, as well as a strong advocacy for the common person. In fact, his signature character was a pencil-thin Everyman forced by the powers-that-be to don only a barrel.

In a Chambers cartoon from 1966, on the occasion of a Federal-

Robert Chambers spent years sharing his satirical views on daily life in Halifax through the local papers.

Provincial Conference on Medicare, Health Minister Allan MacEachen stands in an operating theatre preparing his scalpel on a tool shed file while the provincial premiers scream procedural directions at him from the spectators' gallery. A timeless Canadian theme, the patient is, of course, Chambers' Everyman, anesthetized and too trusting.

One of Chambers' favourite figures was Robert Stanfield, whom he began drawing when Stanfield was still in provincial politics. Towards the end of his career, in a gesture it is difficult to imagine in today's world, Chambers confessed to never having been too hard on Stanfield, as he often ran into him while walking to work down Spring Garden Road. "It would be pretty hard to face him with a bad cartoon in the morning paper," he said. Later he presented Stanfield with a personalized collection of cartoons, which Stanfield promptly donated to the Public Archives of Nova Scotia.

In 1976, Chambers retired his pen and was invested as a member of the Order of Canada.

— *Richard Norman*

GAJINDAR CHOWDHURY
1931-2002
Cremated with ashes scattered at Peggy's Cove

Gajindar Chowdhury.

Gajindar Chowdhury unknowingly made Nova Scotia history when he arrived in Halifax on October 1, 1959. When he stepped off the plane at Shearwater Military Airport, he became the first East Indian to immigrate to the province.

Chowdhury, who was born in Kathmandu, Nepal, in 1931, dreamed of studying in Canada and educational opportunities brought him to Halifax. He studied at Dalhousie University and often acted as an interpreter for Indians immigrating to Canada via Halifax's Pier 21.

The following year, another Indian joined Chowdhury as a permanent resident. In 1961, the Indo-Canadian community became three, and the growth began. In 1963, Chowdhury, along with his father and a handful of Indian immigrants living and working in Halifax, founded an Indian Association to welcome new Indian immigrants and hold social events to stave off homesickness.

Chowdhury was a founder of the Maritime Sikh Society of 10 Parkdale Drive in Halifax. In the early 1970s, he and a group of fellow Sikhs bought land in Armdale to eventually build and operate a place of worship known as a Gurdwara. In 1979, this dream came true and today, in Halifax, the Sikh Gurdwara is the only permanent structure of its kind in Atlantic Canada.

As an elementary school teacher, Chowdhury taught for 25 years in Halifax at some then well-known schools which are now closed, including G. K. Butler, South Armdale, and Central Spryfield. He used to joke with his colleagues that a new teaching assignment numbered that school's years of operation.

For more than 20 years, Chowdhury lived with his family in Clayton Park. After suffering a heart attack, he died on August 7, 2002, in Halifax at the age of 71. He was cremated and, given his love for his adopted home of more than 40 years, his ashes were sprinkled in the Atlantic Ocean near Peggy's Cove.

— *Sanjeev Chowdhury*

EDITH CLAYTON
1920-1989
Buried at East Preston Baptist Church Cemetery

Edith Clayton was a renowned basket weaver who descended from the "refugee blacks" that came to Nova Scotia on British ships during the War of 1812.

Edith Clayton displays a horn of plenty at the Cole Harbour Heritage Farm Museum.

Nearly 1000 of these new immigrants, many with well-developed basket-making skills, came to live in Preston, Nova Scotia. Both men and women participated in this age-old tradition but eventually it became viewed as women's work, albeit an important source of family income.

Clayton, born in nearby Cherry Brook, learned to make baskets as a child from her mother, Selena. Mrs. Clayton, who had six sons and five daughters, and 11 children who died at childbirth, passed on the skill to all the daughters. She also taught many other Nova Scotians through Continuing Education in Dartmouth, demonstrating the "Preston-type basket" throughout the province.

Clayton made her naturally coloured baskets from maple wood, which her husband, Clifford, collected from forest groves. With a "stout jackknife", she shaved long thin strips of various widths of wood to make bassinets, doll's cradles and fishing baskets, and devising new shapes. She learned to work fast, producing several hundred baskets a year to sell at the open-air market on Water Street.

Clayton, who became a regular on the national craft circuit, received much acclaim for her work, representing the province at a crafts event in Ottawa, participating in the 1986 Vancouver Expo, and receiving a medal of honour from Queen Elizabeth II in 1977.

Clayton left a lasting legacy. In the Winter 1982 issue of *Canadian Woman Studies*, Sylvia Hamilton notes that she taught basket making "as a means of preserving and passing on a significant and uniquely Afro-Nova Scotian aspect of the culture and heritage of the province."

— Roma Senn

ANDREW COBB
1876-1943
Buried at All Saints Anglican Cemetery, Bedford

The architecture of Andrew Cobb recently received renewed interest when an early Cobb-designed house in Bedford was threatened with demolition. Built in 1912, the Charles MacCulloch House is an important part of the Cobb design collection in Bedford, the community where Cobb resided for many years.

Cobb was born in 1876 in Brooklyn, New York, to an American father and a mother from Granville Ferry, Nova Scotia. When Cobb was 14 his father died and his mother moved to Greenwich near Wolfville. He attended Horton School and Acadia University before receiving a scholarship to the School of Architecture at the Massachusetts Institute of Technology in Boston. He earned a Bachelor of Science and then a Master of Science in 1904. After working with three architectural firms in Ohio and getting married, he and his wife, Myrtle, sailed to Europe in 1907. There he entered the École des Beaux-Arts in Paris. Two years later, the couple returned to Halifax.

Cobb was a talented, generous and warm-hearted man who did well from the start. With the birth of his first daughter he decided to design his own house in Bedford, which he called Cobbweb I. This was the first of three homes he would build for his family, each with the same whimsical name.

In 1912, Bedford had less than 200 houses and cottages on the entire Bedford Basin. Living there meant a daily commute by train to work, but this suited Cobb well. It was a spiritual home, a place of peace and quiet in the midst of unspoiled nature. Following the birth of their second daughter, he built Cobbweb II. Although Myrtle was less than happy in Bedford, she stayed for the sake of their children. Aside from a brief return to Halifax after 1916, Bedford remained their home for the rest of Cobb's life.

His early homes fit the style categorized as either Craftsman or Classical. The former is characterized by shingles, steep-pitched roofs, dormer windows and large porches or verandas set under the roof overhang. Craftsman

A 1918 Tudor Revival house designed by Andrew Cobb. The style is derived from the half-timbered English cottages and houses of the late 1600s and early 1700s.

houses fit well into the streetscape and could be designed to fit most budgets. Cobb's interior designs were his hallmark, with beamed ceilings, wainscoting and usually fine fireplaces, often with stained and leaded glass built in.

Cobb is also responsible for many fine buildings in Halifax, in particular the Georgian classicism of Dalhousie University and the University of King's College. He also designed the entire town of Corner Brook, Newfoundland.

Cobb had an extraordinary ability to accommodate his clients' wishes, which may explain his life-long popularity as an architect and the enduring success of his buildings.

— *Graeme F. Duffus*

ISABELLA BINNEY COGSWELL

1819-1874
Buried at Camp Hill Cemetery, Halifax

Isabella Cogswell was called a "ministering angel" and she was "one of the most distinguished women Nova Scotia has ever had." Her name is "synonymous with benevolence and good work."

Now known as Victoria Hall, the "Old Ladies Home" on Gottingen Street was one of a number of institutions supported by the philanthropic efforts of Isabella Cogswell.

A well-known philanthropist, Cogswell is remembered for the incredible amount of time, money and energy she devoted to the education of the poor, the improvement of housing, and the care of the orphaned and elderly.

The daughter of government official and Halifax Banking Company founder Henry Hezekiah Cogswell, she was born in Halifax in 1819. Her brother William was a curate at St Paul's Church, and she herself was connected with the church throughout her life. She remained an important part of St Paul's and of the surrounding community until her death in 1874. "She spent her whole time in helping others and gave large sums of money, but she was very retiring," noted the *Acadian Recorder*.

Cogswell founded a large number of charitable institutions, including the Halifax Industrial School, a school for neglected boys, the Old Ladies' Home, the Home for the Aged, St. Paul's Parochial District Visiting Society, and the Halifax branch of the Colonial Church Society. She was a founding member of St. Paul's Alms House of Industry for Girls, established in 1867. The original mandate of the home was the care of girls aged 10 to 14 after which the girls were found suitable employment in local homes. In 1887, St. Paul's Alms House of Industry for Girls was incorporated as a separate entity from the parish and later the name was shortened to St. Paul's Home for Girls. In 1982, the name became simply St. Paul's Home in acknowledgement of the need to assist boys, as well.

Cogswell's legacy lives on through the continued work of St. Paul's Home, which now provides seven homes for youth in need, including Phoenix Shelter, which occupies the original site of St. Paul's Alms House of Industry for Girls on Tower Road in Halifax, and Cogswell House in Sackville.

— *Justine Hart*

ENOS COLLINS
1774-1871

Enos Collins was a major player in the financial, economic and political development of early colonial Nova Scotia. He founded "The Imperial Bank of Commerce" and amassed the greatest fortune in the Dominion of Canada.

Born in Liverpool, Nova Scotia, to a prosperous seafaring family of Yankee origins, Collins started his career as a young cabin boy on one of his father's ships. He soon made great profits as a privateer in the West Indies for the Royal Navy during the Napoleonic Wars. He was famous for running Napoleon's Blockade of Spain and getting crucial supplies through to General Wellington, later the Duke of Wellington.

Collins moved his booming shipping business to Halifax in 1811 and, with his ship the *Liverpool Packet*, captured 50 American merchant ships off the coast of Boston and sold them in Halifax, making millions in profit during the War of 1812. By 1821 he was Nova Scotia's wealthiest citizen, with a grand mansion on Argyle Street, now the historic Carleton House.

This building, which once housed Collins Bank, still stands today in Halifax's Historic Properties.

In 1825, Collins married heiress Margaret Haliburton and established Nova Scotia's first bank — The Halifax Banking Company — that he nicknamed Collins Bank. Later, the name evolved into the Imperial Bank of Commerce. This new bank allowed Collins and his partners to control much of Nova Scotia's economy and politics.

Collins reached his zenith of power in 1827 as the foremost member of the infamous Council of Twelve, which politically ran Nova Scotia, and brought Collins into direct conflict with Nova Scotia's greatest politician and journalist, Joseph Howe. Howe established the Bank of Nova Scotia in 1832 as a successful counter-force to Collins.

When Collins died in 1871 on his Halifax estate in Gorsebrook, he was the richest man in Canada. Collins Bank still stands in Halifax as Canada's oldest bank structure. It is amusing today to remember that the financial gains made from so many millions in privateer booty played such a major role in the founding of these banking empires.

— Allan Doyle

RANDAL DUANE CONNERS
1956-1994
Buried at St. Alban's Columbarium, Cathedral Church of All Saints, Halifax

In 2004, the international spread of AIDS was described by the United Nations as a "global epidemic," affecting more than 39.4 million around the world.

In 1987, AIDS was a far more obscure disease. Randal Conners, a working-class computer programmer and severe hemophiliac, learned he had contracted AIDS through tainted blood. He unknowingly infected his wife Janet with the disease. Both became activists, fighting for compensation and respect for AIDS victims: travelling to Ottawa for press conferences, dropping money and Band-Aids on the floor of the Canadian Red Cross, speaking at rallies and lobbying the federal and provincial governments.

Before activists like the Conners exposed the ubiquitous nature of the disease, AIDS was seen as a "gay problem" — a disease spread by drug addicts and godless miscreants, not something morally upright citizens should be concerned about. In a sense, Conners was the perfect candidate to rally for AIDS victims. He was a down-to-earth straight man who caught the disease through no fault of his own. Regular folks could identify with his plight and through his activism, Conners was able to show that all AIDS victims deserved respectful treatment.

Together the Conners fought for a federal investigation into the blood supply system. He testified in 1993 and told the Krever Inquiry he did not "know who to blame." His fight won a $139-million compensation package from the provinces for more than 1,000 people suffering from AIDS contracted through tainted blood. His work was also instrumental in winning compensation for those who contracted Hepatitis C through blood products. According to Santo Caira, executive director of Hemophilia Ontario, Conners "took on the government establishment and shattered the conspiracy of silence by telling the truth."

In 2001, Conners (posthumously) and his wife, Janet, received meritorious service medals from the Governor General for their AIDS activism. The province of Nova Scotia noted that the couple made Canadian history.

Conners died in his home at the age of 38 of complications from his illness. Janet and college-aged son Gus were at his bedside.

In 1993, less than a year before his death, Conners told *MacLean's* magazine: "I used to worry that when I died no one would remember me. Now, I know that no matter what happens, Janet and I will have left a mark."

— *Chris Arsenault*

PATRICK CONNORS
1828-1909
Buried at Mount Olivet Cemetery, Halifax

A headstone in Mount Olivet Cemetery sacred to the memory of Patrick Connors who died February 11, 1909, at the age of 81, bears a verse:

> When I am dead, and in my grave,
> Please mark the spot with a marble stave,
> So folks will say, there he lies –
> Poor Pat, who made the rods & flies.

Connors had an ordinary life in most respects. He was born in Harbour Grace, Newfoundland, in 1828 to Michael Connors and Elizabeth Hartry. They moved to Halifax a few years later.

In the 1860s, Patrick opened a shop at the foot of Buckingham Street, a street now lost under Scotia Square and the Cogswell Street interchange. It was a small, narrow store consisting of two rooms, one in front of the other, with living space upstairs. The shop was littered with lengths of bamboo and whittlings of wood, pieces of string and canisters filled with hooks and bits of feathers and felt. He used these materials to fashion fishing rods and flies.

Sport fishing was a favourite pursuit of Victorians and for half a century, until shortly before the outbreak of World War I, Connors' shop catered to uniformed and civilian men setting forth to the trout lakes surrounding Halifax.

In 1859 he met Margaret Brackett, from Herring Cove, whom he called Molly. A courtship began and it seemed that a wedding would follow, but the courtship continued for 30 years. Just when it seemed the two would never become one, the priest from St. Mary's was sent for to join them in matrimony.

The clergyman found Connors and another man sitting with Molly's sister. He was ushered into a room where Molly, fatally ill, was propped up in her bed. On February 27, 1889, Patrick and Molly exchanged vows of marriage. Nine days later, Connors was a widower.

Together for thirty years, united for nine days, the couple experienced yet another irony.

Molly was buried in Holy Cross Cemetery on South Park Street, but when Connors died 20 years later, he was interred across town in Mount Olivet Cemetery. Even in death, the lovers were not one.

— *Terrence M. Punch*

HELEN CREIGHTON
1899-1989
Cremated and buried at Mount Herman Cemetery, Dartmouth

When Helen Creighton published her best-selling book *Bluenose Ghosts* people would complain they couldn't sleep after reading it. "That's fine," Creighton would reply. "I couldn't sleep after writing it."

Canada's premier folklorist, Creighton grew up comfortably in Dartmouth as the youngest of six children. Well-educated with a degree in music from McGill University, she attended the Halifax Ladies' College and the Institute of Folklore in Indiana and trained in social work at University of Toronto. She received six honorary degrees.

In 1928, a journalism project for which Creighton collected information on Nova Scotia pirates sparked her interest in folklore. Her work was driven by passion and, in her opinion, destiny. "It didn't seem that all these things could have happened by chance," she said in 1983. It wasn't long before Creighton became Canada's premier folklorist.

Before divided highways, she logged as many as 6,400 kilometres a year on Nova Scotia's back roads gathering folksongs, ghost stories and histories, all with different cultural significance. Her collections span 60 years and represent works from a variety of cultures that were dispersed throughout Nova Scotia, including Gaelic, English, German, African-Nova Scotian, French, Acadian, and Mi'kmaq.

She became known as both tenacious and resourceful. In the days before radio and television, people happily shared their stories with her. "All the treasures were there for the taking," she told *Atlantic Insight* magazine. "They certainly didn't realize how great a treasure it was."

She was known internationally for arranging almost 40,000 different textual, visual and auditory works, making her one of the more esteemed folklore collectors in the world. As the author of 13 books, she documented and preserved stories and myths of Maritime tradition that could easily have been lost forever.

In her travels, she discovered people singing "lost" songs ranging from thirteenth-century ballads to "The Nova Scotia Song" (Farewell to Nova Scotia), which she discovered in the 1930s; it has since become the province's unofficial anthem. She grappled with many different mediums and styles of folklore, including children's stories, proverbs, plays, songs and stories. Her best-known emphasis, however, was on the supernatural, superstitions, ghost stories and witchcraft.

Creighton's long list of achievements include Distinguished Folklorist of 1981, fellow of the American Folklore Society, Honorary Life President of the Canadian Author's Association, the Queen's Medal, and member of the Order of Canada. In addition, to honour her memory the Helen Creighton Foundation and the Helen Creighton Folklore Festival were established.

— Roma Senn and Bridget Arsenault

SAMUEL CUNARD
1787-1865

Samuel Cunard was a visionary who foresaw the day when steam power would replace sail on the North Atlantic. His interest in steam dated back to 1815 when he was one of the original incorporators of the Halifax Steamboat Company, which considered steam to improve the ferry service across Halifax Harbour.

Cunard was born in 1787 in a small cottage off Brunswick Street. He was one of nine children. His parents, Abraham and Margaret (Murphy) Cunard, were United Empire Loyalists who had immigrated to Nova Scotia from Pennsylvania in 1783.

Portrait of Samuel Cunard by American artist Albert G. Hoit, c.1849.

Cunard attended the Halifax Grammar School but was otherwise self-educated. After training as first clerk in the Engineer's Lumberyard in Greenbank, Cunard founded the firm of A. Cunard & Son with his father in 1812 and engaged in timber and West Indies trade. Following his father's death in 1824, he changed the name of the firm to S. Cunard & Company.

Cunard had a magnificent four-storey warehouse, built of ironstone from Purcell's Cove, and wharves on Upper Water Street. It was a constant scene of shipping activity. His fleet once numbered nearly 80, for a time making Cunard the largest owner of wooden sailing vessels in Nova Scotia.

Cunard married Susan Duffus in 1815 and they had nine children. Sadly, Susan died shortly after giving birth to their last child, Elizabeth, in 1828. His mother-in-law helped Cunard raise his family and they regularly attended Saint George's Round Church near the Cunard home on Brunswick Street.

Cunard played an active role in both the commercial and social life in Halifax. He was: captain in the volunteer 2nd Battalion Militia; president of the Sunfire Company, a volunteer fire brigade; president of the local Chamber of Commerce; an original partner in the Halifax Banking Company, one of the initial trustees of the Halifax Whaling Company; a shareholder and later president of the Shubenacadie Canal Company; a Commissioner of Lighthouses for the Province of Nova Scotia; and, for 10 years, served as a Crown-appointed member of the Council of Twelve — 12 influential people chosen from the Halifax establishment to run the affairs of the province.

In 1840, Cunard became the "pioneer of steam navigation" when he successfully introduced steam to the North Atlantic with his first mail steamer *Britannia*, revolutionizing commerce and communication between continents. The name Cunard, forever linked to Halifax, birthplace of the company founder, endures to this day aboard the *Queen Mary 2*, the new flagship of the Cunard Line.

— *John Langley*

DONALD CURREN
1923-1996
Buried at Brookside Cemetery, Bedford

Donald Curren spent most of his life trying to improve conditions for disabled persons. Born in 1923 in Bedford, where he received his early schooling, he later attended the former Bloomfield High School in Halifax. He grew up on the Curren family farm on Dartmouth Road overlooking

Bedford Basin, where his family ran the Hillcrest Dairy, which supplied the citizens of Bedford and the surrounding area.

Curren worked 15 months with the Department of Veterans Affairs before enlisting in the Royal Canadian Air Force at the age of 18. In 1943, his plane crashed during take-off near Bournsmouth, England, leaving him paralyzed from the waist down, instantly changing his life.

Following years of hospitalization in England and later in Canada, Curren returned to Nova Scotia and received his law degree in 1950 from Dalhousie University and was admitted to the Nova Scotia Bar the following year. During his hospitalization in Halifax, Curren met Joan Ellis, an occupational therapist from Kitchener, Ontario, whom he married in 1947. They adopted two sons.

Donald Curren (seated) and friends attend a Bedford Central School reunion.

Curren never practised law. In 1947, he was named the Maritime representative to the Canadian Paraplegic Association (CPA) and, after his bar admission, was asked to serve a five-year term as executive director of its Nova Scotia division, which he had earlier founded. He served this organization for 32 years, retiring in 1984.

"We are only passing through life once," he said, "and if we can't leave a place better for having been there then our contribution has not been much." His dedication lead to many improvements for all Nova Scotians: a new building code, seatbelt legislation, curb cutaways, improved transportation and designated parking.

He received many awards: he was made a Queen's Counsel in 1974, received two Community Services Awards, and became a member of the Order of Canada. He held honorary degrees from Dalhousie and Saint Mary's universities.

John Rogers, Curren's successor at the CPA, said: "I have not seen dedication like that in any other man I have known."

— *C. Nelson Kennedy*

WILLIAM EDGAR DEGARTHE
1907-1983
Ashes interred in the William deGarthe monument, Peggy's Cove

Next to the deGarthe Art Gallery in Peggy's Cove stands a spectacular 30-metre granite monument that William deGarthe carved to honour the fishermen of Nova Scotia.

William Edward deGarthe, a well-known Nova Scotian painter, sculptor and writer, was born Birger Edward Degerstedt in Kasko, Finland, and was one of five sons. Following graduation, he was conscripted into a military academy. In the army, he sent home outrageous cartoons depicting "lampoons of army life." After completing his army tour, deGarthe, then 19, decided to visit an aunt in Brazil.

When deGarthe's ship docked in Halifax he was short of funds, and he went to the backwoods of Ontario to cut down trees. After two months of this strenuous labour, he decided to move on. In Montreal, he worked as an illustrator, making seven dollars a week. While waiting for his ship to return to Halifax, he met the owner of an advertising company who offered him a job.

In 1935, deGarthe met and married Phoebe Agnes Payne, settled in Timberlea near Halifax and established an advertising business. He also con-

The Fishermen's Monument, carved by William deGarthe: a monument to those who live and work upon the Atlantic, and deGarthe's final resting place.

tinued to study his own art. His wife encouraged him to become a full-time artist. Many of their friends were artists and as a group they would paint at Peggy's Cove. He also became known for his sculptures and went to Italy to the same place Leonardo da Vinci studied to learn this art form.

Through his paintings and sculptures, people have come to know Peggy, believed to be the only survivor of a shipwreck on the rocks of Peggy's Cove. According to folklore, the locals saved Peggy, who was on her way to meet her fiancé. People would often go to visit "Peggy at the Cove," thus giving it her name. This tale has grown over the years. DeGarthe was often heard saying he could see her ghostly figure standing on the rocks searching for her lost love while surrounded by a foggy mist, and that is how he painted her. Eventually, deGarthe's love for the small fishing village convinced him to move there permanently.

After deGarthe died in 1983, his wife offered their home and the monument to the Nova Scotia government, which agreed to construct an art gallery to house his artwork. Today, countless tourists flock to Peggy's Cove and visit the William deGarthe monument, a lasting memorial to a fine artist.

— *Alfreda Withrow*

GEORGE N. DELEFES
1914-1944
Buried at Camp Hill Cemetery, Halifax

The Greek merchant ship SS *Aikaterini T.* sank in heavy seas somewhere southeast of Brier Island, Digby County, in the early morning hours on January 24, 1944, with the loss of all 26 crewmen. The last communication from the ship, a request for W/T bearings, was heard from Yarmouth at about 1:00 a.m. That signal was sent by George Delefes, the ship's wireless officer. His body washed ashore at Central Grove on the north shore of

George Delefes, c.1942.

Long Island. The bodies of 12 other crewmembers were recovered along the Bay of Fundy at such places as Tiverton, Whale Cove and Church Point.

George Delefes was born in Smyrna, Turkey, in 1914. At the time of his birth he was registered as a Greek citizen in Heraklion, Crete, to avoid later conscription into the Turkish forces. In 1922, the Delefes family, along with more than a million other Greeks living in Asia Minor, fled Turkey in advance of the destruction of Smyrna by the Turks. The family settled in Athens, Greece.

After high school, Delefes enrolled in a three-year program to qualify as a marine wireless operator. He arrived in Halifax in 1941, and resided in the city while not at sea.

After Greece had been occupied by the Germans in 1941, many ships of the Greek merchant marine such as the *Aikaterini T.* came to North America, providing coastal shipping service and overseas convoy duty throughout the war. Sometime in 1941, the *Aikaterini T.* arrived in Halifax. At a social event hosted by St. George's Greek Orthodox Church, then situated at the corner of Morris and Queen Streets, Delefes met Lilyan Karas, and after a brief courtship, they married on June 3, 1942. Lilyan resided at 38 Morris Street where her parents, James and Mary, operated a fruit and confectionary business. Following their marriage, they took up residence with the Karas family above their store on the corner of Morris and Barrington Streets.

In the summer of 1942, Delefes was asked to manage a hostel for Greek seamen in Lunenburg for the Greek merchant marine. He and his wife moved to Lunenburg to supervise the hostel, the Ich Dien Inn. Unfortunately, the seamen, who were on shore leave, were not happy in Lunenburg where there were few opportunities to socialize during the war years. After functioning for a brief period, the Inn closed and Delefes returned to Halifax whereupon he was reassigned to the *Aikaterini T.*

On January 22, 1944, Delefes left Halifax on the *Aikaterini T.'s* fateful trip. Bound for Saint John, New Brunswick, the ship was carrying a cargo of coal from Louisburg. To this day the cause of the ship's sinking is uncertain.

— *Peter Delefes*

ROBERT MATTHIAS DIETZ
1914-1999
Cremated in Halifax

Born in Mayen, Germany, into an innkeeping family in 1924, Robert Matthias Dietz claimed he was "the result of my father's love for music and my mother's artistic talents." Drafted into the army at 18, Dietz served as a gunner in Italy and on the Russian front. Captured at Kustrin, he escaped

Robert Dietz.

and immigrated to Canada. He arrived at Pier 21 on December 12, 1951, with a trumpet, a suitcase and no money.

He set off to find people who made music, playing French horn in the Stadacona and Royal Canadian Artillery bands, and then became general manager of the Halifax Symphony. He was the driving force behind the creation of the Atlantic Symphony Orchestra, which he managed as well. It was the first regional symphony orchestra in Canada.

Dietz's next step took him to Saint Mary's University Art Gallery as director and father confessor to many students. He became an ardent critic of culture in Nova Scotia. "This is so schtupid," Dietz would say on the latest absurdity in the arts, followed by a burst of laughter.

In 1978, Robert founded Dresden Galleries. Here one could hear the latest news on the arts and the best gossip in town while enjoying the coffee, schnapps and brandy that Dietz always had on hand. If someone liked a painting and had no money, he'd say: "Take it! Hang it on your wall! Enjoy it! Pay me when you can." He encouraged and supported young and emerging artists, giving many of them their first exhibition, and organized two showings of sacred art in Halifax. The gallery miraculously survived until 1990.

Dietz, however, did not retire. He organized exhibitions and painted his war experiences in Expressionist style. He wrote his autobiography *Oath of Allegiance* in 1992, the play *Gunner Schmidt at the Crossroads* in 1994, and a book for teachers called *Art is Not a Dessert* in 1996. For Dietz, art offered the perfect antidote to war, fear and hatred: "For where there is music there is no war."

He died of a stroke in 1999. At a celebration of his life on August 4, rich with music and readings from Dietz's much-loved poet Rainer Maria Rilke, a young friend summed up the essence of the life of this deeply spiritual man: "You taught me idealism and truth. You cared for people — and they cared back."

— *Jim Lotz*

ROSA DIMATTIA
1909-1998
Buried in Gates of Heaven Cemetery, Lower Sackville

In the 1960s, Rosa DiMattia arrived in Halifax at Pier 21 from Castelbasso, Italy, and encouraged a large number of Italians to immigrate to Canada.

Born in 1909, Rosa was the daughter of Maria and Amadio DiGiacinto, neighbours of the wealthy DiMattia family. She was known as a hard worker and, at 15, she ably and calmly helped deliver a neighbour's baby while working in the fields. Afterwards, the doctor would often call on Rosa for help. She took a midwife's course and became the midwife for her village and the surrounding towns, delivering several hundred babies.

When Rosa fell in love with the neighbours' son, Massimo DiMattia, the couple was forbidden from seeing each other, but they secretly wrote each other letters, hiding them in an olive tree. Unfortunately, Rosa's older brother Vincenzo caught her and felt compelled to tell their parents. Although it was unacceptable for an Italian landowner's son to court a "land worker's daughter," they eventually received reluctant permission to marry.

Rosa's mother-in-law did not accept her until she proved herself. When Massimo contracted tuberculosis, the doctor prescribed medication that was

Rosa DiMattia displays the 137-metre scarf she knitted.

only available in Teramo, a 33-kilometre walk from their village, and Rosa walked there and back for the medicine. When she returned, the doctor gave her another prescription and, without hesitation, she ventured out again. This time, she did not have enough money to buy the medication and had to sell the beautiful necklace her husband gave her on their wedding day. This act convinced Rosa's mother-in-law that her heart was true.

Although Massimo recovered, he died circa 1955 from a heart attack, which forced Rosa to run the family's business. She continued to support her family and land workers, but life was tough after World War II and she considered immigrating to Canada. She convinced her older brother, who had already moved to Canada, to sponsor their cousin and a friend. During the next 10 years, she encouraged many Italians to immigrate, and often provided them the necessary funds herself. Rosa finally left Italy and travelled to Canada with her son, Dante. They were sponsored by Rosa's married daughter, Victoria.

When she arrived in Halifax, she could not speak any English. She sat in on the primary class at Oxford School, where she was loved by the children and accepted as a student.

In 1986, she started knitting a beautiful, multicoloured scarf that eventually reached 137 metres. The scarf was featured on a segment of *Sesame Street*, the popular children's television program.

On Rosa's 75th birthday, Dante presented her with a replica of the necklace she had sold to purchase the medicine that saved her husband's life. Her name has been inscribed on a plaque at Pier 21 and she is remembered for her many good works.

— *Alfreda Withrow*

GEORGE DIXON
1870-1909

George Dixon was once the most famous black man in the world — a boxing champion renowned for his skill and courage. Today, almost a century after his death, he remains a cultural icon in Halifax, where his life's story became a musical, a community centre bears his name and his prize-fighting career is both galvanizing spirit and cautionary tale.

Born in 1870, the photographer's apprentice from Africville was the first black to win a world boxing championship when he captured the bantamweight (115 pounds) title in 1890. When Dixon won the featherweight (122 pounds) championship in 1892, he became the first man of any colour to hold more than two world titles at the same time. In addition, Little

George Dixon, born in Africville, was an international boxing champion.

Chocolate, as he became known, was one of the most innovative prize-fighters ever, credited with inventing shadow boxing and the suspended punching bag. He was inducted into the International Boxing Hall of Fame in 1990.

Dixon won 130 of 158 recorded professional fights. Scores were gruelling affairs. (In 1890 he fought to a 70-round draw in Boston; then five months later in New York, he beat the same man in 22 rounds.) He earned thousands of dollars for his high-profile matches — amounts previously unknown outside the heavyweight division. He also collected considerable sums from side-bets during hundreds of "barnstorming" exhibitions in towns across North America and in England. These bareknuckle fights often lasted for at least 20 rounds against local challengers in backrooms and beer halls where patrons cared little that what they were watching was actually the most brilliant ring strategist of his generation. Often spectators spewed racial slurs, burned his skin with cigars and whacked his legs with billy clubs. More than once he left the ring via police escort.

Dixon was also a controversial social figure for his era. After moving to Boston early in his career, he married the sister of his white promoter, a marriage that enraged both races.

Despite his ring success and large purses, his end was inglorious. At age 38, on a frigid January day in 1909, Dixon was found delirious in a New York alley, wearing only old boxing trunks, fists bleeding from punching locked doors. Addicted to alcohol and opium, he died of exposure a few days later, penniless.

— Robert Ashe

PAT DOHERTY
1941-1991
Buried at Gates of Heaven Cemetery, Lower Sackville

Passing my soon-to-be-read, hi-fi magazine to the man behind the counter at Atlantic News on Morris Street back in 1977, I was startled as it was snatched from my hand. The man's face jutted out as he almost yelled out the words: "What kind of hi-fi do you have? No holding back, now! Spit it out, boy!"

Pat Doherty.

Thus I met Pat Doherty, proprietor of Atlantic News, the best magazine store in the city of Halifax and everywhere else I traveled over the next 14 years, often on vacation with him and his wife, Onough.

What better place to ambush likely fellow travelers than his store, where folks could indulge their interests in more than 2,000 appropriate magazine titles. Then, after a quick quiz to assess whether you had the brainpower to understand his passions, Doherty co-opted you to join a club, give a lecture, complete a task, or merely banter with his mind — the quickest mind I ever met on any subject at all.

Doherty, who was born in Halifax, was an outstanding student who competed in a regular general-knowledge radio show. In the 1950s, he won a scholarship to Saint Mary's High School, located at the university's current site, where he also graduated. He had an interest in many things, almost all of them machinery- and equipment-related such as motorcycles, radio-control model cars and hi-fi, in addition to cats (the feline variety).

Folks were drawn into his web. There were no half-measures — he made you perform. Every day, he woke up with a list of tasks to be tackled that day and not the next, and he accomplished them all. In his eyes, you were expected to do the same.

In 1982, *Atlantic Insight* magazine listed Doherty, "the amiable proprietor," as one of the great things about Halifax.

He died of cancer at 47. At his overflowing funeral I met strangers who regarded Pat as their best friend. That was the measure of a unique man, the like of which I've never met before or since.

— Bruce Armstrong

ANDREW DOWNS
1811–1892
Buried at St. John's Anglican Cemetery, Fairview

Andrew Downs was born in New Jersey in 1811 to Robert Downs, an illiterate Scottish tinsmith (plumber), and Elizabeth Plum. Even before the family moved to Halifax in 1825, the boy was fascinated with nature. In 1833, he met and was inspired by John James Audubon, with whom he corresponded afterwards.

He was a plumber and active in the Halifax Mechanics' Institute, a young, deft and painstaking workman. Downs proposed in 1838 that Halifax establish a park, museum and library of natural history. In 1847, he began to acquire land near the head of the Northwest Arm as a site on which to realize his dream of a zoological garden in Halifax. Twenty years later, his *Walton*

Andrew Downs stands in front of his glass house and aviary.

(named for the estate of naturalist Charles Waterton, which he had visited) consisted of 127 acres with a greenhouse, an aviary, an aquarium and his "Gothic Cottage," a cathedral of glass. Edward, Prince of Wales, visited the gardens, and Victor Emanuel II of Italy heard of Down's skill as a taxidermist and engaged him to mount hunting trophies.

When New York's Central Park lured Downs to become superintendent of its zoological collections in 1867, he sold his zoo. But political manoeuvring obliged him to return to Armdale shortly afterwards. He tried for three years to re-establish his zoo, but lack of support and vandalism dampened his hopes. In 1872 he abandoned his dream, and Halifax lost its chance of having the first zoological gardens in America since those of the Aztec emperor Montezuma in Mexico, 350 years earlier.

On the practical side, Downs trained pigeons for use to communicate with Sable Island and bred prize-winning poultry. After Titus Smith's death (1850), visitors who wanted to learn about wildlife in the woods and by the waters of Acadia went to Downs for advice or reference.

Downs lived his final years on Agricola Street at the corner of May, mounting animals for collectors and writing papers on ornithology. He died at home on August 26, 1892, aged almost 81. After his death, a friend wrote that he was one "whose heart was in his work, if ever man's was, and who had the liberality of spirit which all true lovers of nature have." There is a monument to Downs and his gardens not far above the Armdale Rotary on what is now Joseph Howe Drive.

— *Terrence M. Punch*

THOMAS DRYDEN
DATES UNKNOWN

Thomas Dryden was one of the Eastern Shore's most colourful characters.

Following the American Revolution (1775-1783), a group of disbanded soldiers and their families sailed from Halifax to Antigonish. A violent storm arose and the vessel took shelter in Beaver Harbour. The bad weather persisted and the captain, who had been instructed to return to Halifax as soon as possible, disembarked his 174 passengers who were required to spend the winter there. In May 1784, the group was picked up and transported to Antigonish.

Dryden was in this group.

Although he received a grant of 100 acres at Bay St. Lawrence, Antigonish County, Dryden returned to Beaver Harbour, because this community is given as Thomas and Elizabeth Dryden's residence when their daughter was baptized in 1795.

However, the Dryden family left Beaver Harbour and moved to Liscomb.

When Dryden, a poor fisherman, stepped onboard the *Leander* in 1817 in Liscomb Harbour to petition for land, Lieutenant-Governor Dalhousie was on the vessel. The *Dalhousie Journals* (edited by Marjorie Whitelaw) vividly captures Dalhousie's impressions of the event. Dryden, now a father of 11 children, petitioned for a grant of land on which he had resided for approximately 15 years.

Dalhousie had noted that Dryden had long, lanky white hair that covered his old wrinkled head. He wore a ragged hat, which was sewn together with rope yarn; a flannel shirt with red and yellow patches, and a pair of soldier's old pantaloons. Dalhousie noted that Dryden did not wear shoes. But to everyone's surprise, this pathetic-looking fisherman spoke perfect Latin and Greek. Dryden informed Dalhousie that he came from a good Irish family and had been educated at Trinity College, Dublin, and that he had run away from home, enlisted in the British army, fought in the American Revolution and had been a captive in Philadelphia for three years during the war. He also

Dryden's Cove at Port Dufferin, N.S., c.1940.

told Dalhousie that "he had in his day spent a great deal of money. He had sown a plentiful store of wild oats, and reaped his crop of Misery." Dryden's visit concluded after Admiral David Milne gave him a bag of biscuits and the sailors gave him clothes. Dalhousie's parting observation was "he went away as drunk as he well could be."

— Philip Hartling

BESSIE EGAN
1859-1937
Buried in Camp Hill Cemetery, Halifax

Bessie Egan spent her life working with poor women and children in Halifax, and became one of the first female police officers in the city.

Born in Hants County in 1859, Elizabeth (Bates) Egan was adopted by a Halifax family early in life. As a domestic servant in the old north end, she joined the Halifax branch of the Woman's Christian Temperance Union (WCTU) as a charter member in 1881. Her marriage in 1884 did not keep her out of either the paid or volunteer workforce. While she was matron of the WCTU home and coffee rooms on the corner of Sackville and Grafton streets between 1892 and 1902, she also acted as a parochial visitor for St. Paul's Anglican Church and began a life-long association with the church's Girls' Friendly Society and Women's Missionary Auxiliary.

In 1904, after the WCTU closed its doors, Egan took on three new paid jobs: agent for the Society for the Prevention of Cruelty, which rescued children and women and prosecuted all forms of cruelty and neglect; visitor for the Association for Improving the Condition of the Poor, which provided relief for "deserving" poor people; and immigrant agent, tenement and jail visitor for the Nova Scotia Bible Society, whose literature she distributed. In her spare time, she participated in the multi-faceted activities of the Local Council of Women.

The appropriation of welfare and child protection by professional social workers during the First World War encouraged Egan to join the police force in 1917. With her colleague May Virtue, appointed in 1918, Egan intervened in domestic, juvenile, and female cases and exercised the power of arrest over men as well as women. Her energy inspired Ernest H. Blois, provincial director of child welfare, to comment: "Mrs. Egan is a tremendous worker. We have known her to leave Halifax on the morning train for Sydney, returning on that night's train to Halifax, but not in a sleeper, preferring to sit up all night and be on duty all the following day in Halifax."

In 1924, Egan took pride — at least briefly — in the establishment of a closed women's courtroom to protect female prisoners from the public gaze; the magistrate's reliance on the policewomen for suggestions of humane solutions in cases of female vagrancy, prostitution and marital conflict; and the confidence expressed by the Local Council of Women in 1927 when it suggested that Halifax policewomen should have province-wide jurisdiction. However, being employed in a hitherto male occupation did not mean equality. The policewomen received the lowest salaries in the department, less even than new male recruits to the force. On her retirement in 1934, Egan was denied a pension because she was a woman. Only the intervention of powerful patrons secured her support from the city.

Her passing in 1937 occasioned many glowing tributes.

— *Judith Fingard*

PRISCILLA EVANS
1924-2000
Buried in Gates of Heaven Cemetery, Lower Sackville

Priscilla Evans was the lady next door; the neighbourhood gardener who shared her raspberries; the eccentric who wrote notes to herself. But she also had a passion for music, especially early music. She believed that music enriched everyone's life, that it was not just for the gifted or affluent, and it should be affordable, engaging and challenging. Her ability to inspire thousands of Haligonians to make music a part of their lives made her truly extraordinary.

Priscilla Evans.

Born Marjorie Priscilla Lobley in Mount Royal, Quebec, in 1924, Evans began studying piano at the age of four. Her formal training continued at McGill University, where she studied music theory and composition as part of her Honours BA in English. Shortly after her marriage to Maurice Evans, a naval architect and engineer, in 1950, she became a permanent resident of Halifax.

Evans began teaching recorder and music theory in the late 1950s, when few suitable instructional materials were available. Undaunted, she wrote and published four recorder method books, began amassing what eventually became an extensive library of early music, composed and arranged countless instrumental pieces, organized annual student concerts and prepared students for music festivals.

Many musicians played a role in promoting the performance of early music in Halifax, but none greater than Evans. She established The Oxford Players in 1977, dedicated to recorder teaching and performance, and was a founding member of the Early Music Society of Nova Scotia in 1978. In addition, she was instrumental in the establishment of both Mercredi, a group that performed on an assortment of medieval and renaissance instruments, and an amateur viol consort. Many Haligonians heard their first krumhorn, bass recorder or viola da gamba during benefit concerts performed by these groups in the historic Little Dutch Church. Despite her exhausting schedule, Evans also found time to persuade likely candidates that they, too, could play the viola da gamba, offering free lessons and the loan of an instrument and bow as incentives. Halifax now has the largest active amateur viol consort in Canada.

Despite suffering a stroke in the fall of 1999, Evans devoted herself to preparing her students for the February Kiwanis Music Festival. Sadly, she fell ill shortly after the festival's conclusion and died of leukemia less than two weeks later. Her memorial service, held in the recently restored St. George's Round Church, included performances by both Mercredi and a consort of seven viols.

The enormous legacy left by Evans goes beyond the thousands of students she taught over the years. The Early Music Society opened the Priscilla Evans Early Music Library in 2002, and her delightful recorder method books are still available through this organization. No one has yet come forward to fill the teaching void left by her passing.

— *Margaret Holgate*

VINCENT FERGUSON
1906-1984
Buried at Gates of Heaven Cemetery, Lower Sackville

Vincent Ferguson, an outstanding 1930s athlete in hockey, is best known for his 1934–35 season with the Halifax Wolverines hockey team, Maritime Senior Champions who later clinched the prestigious Allan Cup, symbolic of Canadian senior hockey supremacy that attracted as much attention then as today's Stanley Cup.

Ferguson, who was born in Halifax, was an all-star winger. During the semi-final round of the Allan Cup against the Montreal Royals, he scored the tying goal to send the game into three scoreless overtime periods. In the first game of the series against the Montreal Royals, the fans were filing out the doors, conceding the Royals a 3–2 victory, when Ferguson trudged down centre ice and snapped a rainbow shot from far outside the blue line. To the

Vincent Ferguson.

surprise of the huge crowd, the puck slipped slowly into the Montreal net. The Wolverines won that series and went on to defeat the Port Arthur Bearcats in the finals. Ferguson's "Million Dollar Goal" was the turning point in the Wolverine's run to the Allan Cup and became a part of Halifax's hockey lore.

Ferguson, the father of three children, was married to Gertrude Butler and spent 40 years working for Nova Scotia Light and Power. He also played senior baseball with several Halifax teams, including St. Agnes of the Twilight League and the Halifax Shipyards of the Halifax Defense League. A faultless fielder and dangerous base runner, he was feared by opposing pitchers for his ability to hit their best curve balls and fastballs. Year after year, he led the Twilight League as the top batsman.

Ferguson was superstitious and followed a series of rituals that only he knew. He was always on the lookout to see that other members of his team did not draw the wrath of the sporting gods by crossing bats or breaking other taboos. Ferguson is an original member of the Nova Scotia Sport Hall of Fame.

— *Stephen Coutts*

SADIE FINEBERG
1899-1982
Buried at Beth Israel Cemetery, Halifax

When we arrived in Halifax at Pier 21 on March 7, 1939, Sadie Fineberg was there to greet us with tissues to wipe the children's noses and bread in case anyone was hungry. She represented the Jewish Immigrant Aid Society, meeting refugees and immigrants at Pier 21. A kind, compassionate and generous woman, she made you feel at ease right away and took away the strangeness of entering a new country.

When Sadie settled us in a boarding house, she told my mother she would send her two sons to take my sister and me to a show. We spoke no English and they spoke no German, but as children ranging in age from 11 to 15, we got along and overcame the language barrier.

The Finebergs, including Sadie's husband Morris and their three children, became our close friends. They often visited our farm in Milford Station, and we frequently visited their home on Shirley Street. Sadie's home was open to everyone. She was a hospitable woman and, together with her husband, they welcomed servicemen, women and newcomers.

Sadie formed the Shirley Street Group, which was composed of neighbourhood women who volunteered and supported the war effort. For many years,

Sadie Fineberg welcomes new immigrants to Halifax at Pier 21.

she headed the Women's B'nai B'rith, which supported racial and religious tolerance. Halifax was less open then, and Jews were not welcome everywhere.

Frequently, she took her nieces and two daughters-in-law for tea at Woods' Tea Room. I was privileged to be one of them because, in 1946, I married her nephew, Lawrence Ferguson. Aunt Sadie was the family matriarch, and we all looked to her for advice. No family function was celebrated without Aunt Sadie and her family.

Later on, Sadie stopped meeting immigrants for the Jewish Immigrant Society because Halifax's mayor at the time asked her to represent him at Pier 21. She held this position until the Pier closed in the 1970s. My mother, Meta Echt, assumed her former position.

Sadie, who will always be remembered with love and respect, is commemorated in a video at Pier 21 called *Sadie's Pier*, which is shown continually for visitors.

— *Marianne Ferguson*

JOHN FORTUNATO
1912-1990
Buried at Gates of Heaven Cemetery, Lower Sackville

Editor's note: The original version of this article appeared in the February 28, 1990 issue of the *Halifax Daily News*.

Boo! Hiss! Kill the umpire! The baseball game was about to begin and the fans in Stellarton, Nova Scotia, were in their usual festive mood — combative and potentially ugly.

Rather than ignore the catcalls, the umpire turned to face the crowd, pulled off his mask and turned on the world's biggest smile. The mouth in the moon face didn't have 88 keys, it only seemed that way. Immediately the mob was on his side. "Yeah Fotch, you're the best!"

And he was.

Johnny Fortunato may well have been the only umpire extant the fans

John Fortunato.

would pay to see and stay to cheer. And they cheered from the day he arrived from Lewiston, Maine, in 1947 until the day the Halifax and District League folded its tents forever in 1959. And they continued cheering until six years later when The Fotch finally put away his shoes as a basketball referee.

Trite as it may be to say it, The Fotch was a character. He could have stepped straight out of the pages of Damon Runyon. He liked to say he was "a bum with a touch of class." Some would argue with both parts of that self-assessment. He was a throwback to another era, one less fastidious, one less prone to taking offence than our own.

Exuding charm and bonhomie, his conversation was studded with words like "wop" and "hebe" and "dago" and "nigger" — this from a man who was a highly respected social worker in East Preston. Women were invariably "broads," and the better ones were "swell broads."

Memories abound.

The year is 1975, and the provincial government is hosting a luncheon for the athletes appearing that evening at the annual Kingsmeadows' dinner. Garnet Brown, the chairman, asks Fortunato to say the grace. "Dear Lord, thanks for what we're about to receive, compliments of the Honourable A. Garnet Brown, Minister of Recreation, Province of Nova Scotia. Just think, Dear Lord we could be like Babe Ruth — 25 years dead. Amen."

Brown, ever quick, responds: "Thanks, John, that's a true sportsman's grace."

Fortunato, who attended Boston College, said: "Sending me to college was like putting cologne on a pig."

The Fotch loved his adopted province, and his adopted province loved him. At a reunion of the Halifax and District League, several months before he died, he was in the finest form, singing "Southie (Boston) is my home town," and then tearfully saying how good Nova Scotia had been to him. He received one of only two standing ovations that evening.

— Harry Flemming

MICHAEL FRANCKLIN
C. 1733-1782
Buried within St. Paul's Church, Halifax

Michael Francklin was loved and hated. Historians have called the merchant and politician "a puppet," not to mention "pompous, arrogant and incompetent." But he was influential with the Mi'kmaq and the Acadians and is considered one of the truly important founders of the province.

As the fourth child and the second son, Francklin, who was born in

England, moved to Halifax in 1752 because he had no chance to get ahead at home. The town was then "reputed the most wicked in North America," notes Thomas Raddall in *Halifax: Warden of the North*. Francklin sold liquor on George Street and got rich supplying the British forces with fish and rum during the Seven Years' War. He was strongly connected with the notorious Joshua Mauger, a merchant and slave trader. Francklin was a "good looking, wealthy and accomplished young merchant-bachelor, the catch of the town," wrote Raddall. He made a powerful match by marrying Susannah Boutineau of Boston, the granddaughter of Peter Faneuil, a wealthy American colonial merchant. They built an elegant house in what is now downtown Halifax. However, Francklin was usually short of money as he invested nearly every shilling he had in land.

In 1754, a Mi'kmaq band captured Francklin and took him to the Gaspé. During his three months of captivity, Francklin, who could speak French, learned the Mi'kmaq language and developed a respect for Indian culture. Twenty-three years later, he was uniquely qualified to become the Superintendent of Indian Affairs.

From 1766 until 1776, Francklin took on the role of Lieutenant Governor and allowed those Acadians who returned after the expulsion to settle the Minas Basin on terms far more generous than the Council had recommended.

Francklin died in his office on Granville Street in the arms of some Mi'kmaq chiefs, whom Francklin was supplying with clothing and blankets for the winter. During his funeral 200 native Americans followed his coffin to St. Paul's Church, uttering a death chant for a warrior.

— *Roma Senn*

CHARLES FREDERICK FRASER

1850-1925
Buried at Camp Hill Cemetery, Halifax

When Charles Frederick Fraser injured his eye in 1857 while whittling a stick at the age of seven, his father Dr. Benjamin Fraser made every effort to get his fourth son the best medical attention available. A renowned Boston eye specialist refused to operate on such a young child and, as a result, the injury affected the sight in Fraser's other eye. Ultimately, his sight began to fade, ending his father's hope that he would pursue medicine.

Fraser was born on January 4, 1850, and was one of 15 children. His mother, Elizabeth, named him after her brother, Charles Frederick Allison, the founder of Mount Allison Academy, now Mount Allison University in Sackville, New Brunswick.

While Charles was at the Perkins Institute, successful merchant William Murdock from Halifax died in London, bequeathing funds for the establishment of an asylum for the blind in Halifax. In 1871, the Halifax Asylum for the Blind opened with four students and two teachers. Fraser, who returned to Windsor, Nova Scotia, blind, accepted the appointment as first superintendent in 1873 and stayed in that position for the next 50 years. He not only gained honours and advances for the blind but for himself as well.

Riding the wave of altruism that swept across Canada in the later nineteenth century, Superintendent Fraser travelled the Atlantic region with a group of students lecturing and entertaining in smaller communities, gathering interest, funding and new students. By 1883, he had the school's name changed by dropping "asylum." He also secured free postage for books in Braille and successfully fought for free education for the blind. A year later, he began a six-year stint as editor of *The Critic*, a weekly journal of commercial and general news published by his brother, A. Milne Fraser.

In 1891, he married Ella Jane Hunter, a teacher at the School for the Blind who wrote children's stories. Ella Jane's health was poor and she died in 1909, leaving Charles sad and lonely. Soon though, Jane Stevens, of Brooklyn, Nova Scotia, captured his heart and they married in 1910.

He was called to the Bar of the House in 1913 and received public gratitude from the Nova Scotia House of Assembly for 40 years of service to the blind. In June of 1915, he was made Knight Bachelor by King Edward VII. Still he found time for business, public life and quiet summers at "Farraline," his Bedford home on the shore of the Basin which was named for the place of his ancestors in Scotland. In 1918, he founded the Canadian National Institute for the Blind.

— Tony Edwards

CLARENCE GOSSE
1912–1996
Buried at Fairview Cemetery, Halifax

Clarence Gosse, who was born in Newfoundland in 1912, came to Halifax at an early age. After attending medical school at Dalhousie University and finishing post-graduate studies in surgery and urology in Ohio, Dr. Gosse served in the Canadian Medical Corporation. On D-Day he led one of the first surgical units onto the Normandy beaches, performing surgery while under heavy fire and bombardment.

Clarence Gosse unveils a plaque commemorating Samuel Cunard on the Halifax Waterfront.

Upon his return to Halifax, he became head of the Urology Department at both the Camp Hill and Victoria General hospitals, and entered private practice with Dr. Gordon Mack, with whom he had a long-lasting partnership and friendship.

During the 1960s, he led a full and generous public life as chairman of the United Appeal and President of the Nova Scotia Human Rights Commission, among other organizations devoted to the public good.

In 1973, Dr. Gosse became the Lieutenant-Governor of Nova Scotia. Three years later, he played host to Queen Elizabeth II as she made a three-day stopover in Halifax as part of an official trip to Canada for the opening of the Summer Olympics in Montreal.

In the early 1970s, when geologists suspected oil reserves were present off Sable Island, questions were raised over whether the jurisdiction of the island fell under the auspices of the federal or provincial government. Dr. Mack recalled Lieutenant-Governor Gosse leading an unofficial landing party to Sable Island soon after the controversy broke, in an attempt to settle the dispute once and for all. With a number of prominent individuals in attendance, Dr. Gosse planted the old "blue-and-white" in Sable Island's sand, proclaiming the pony sanctuary and the erstwhile oil the eternal property of

Nova Scotia. The federal government was forced to enter into negotiations.

In his later years, Dr. Gosse was named an Officer of the Order of Canada and received a number of honorary degrees from Atlantic Canadian universities.

— Richard Norman

JOHN HALIBURTON
1740-1808
Buried at the Old Burying Grounds, Halifax

John Haliburton was born in Haddington, Scotland, circa 1740. As a young man he trained to be a surgeon. He successfully passed examinations set by the Company of Surgeons of London in 1758, 1760 and 1761, and in the latter year joined the Royal Navy. During the early 1760s, Haliburton served as surgeon's mate and later as surgeon on several Royal Navy frigates. Sometime prior to 1767, however, he was posted to the Naval Yard in Newport, Rhode Island.

In 1773, Haliburton accepted the appointment of surgeon and agent to the Sick and Hurt Board at Newport. Five years later he was appointed surgeon in charge of the Rhode Island Naval Hospital. He continued there until April 12, 1782, when — as he stated in his claim to the Loyalist Claims Commission — "he was obliged to flee in the night leaving his wife, family, and estate." He escaped in a small open boat across Newport Harbour and eventually made his way to the British lines. His affidavit sent to the Claims Commission stated that he had "been sending intelligence of the movements of the French fleet" to the British. The rebel forces discovered that he was spying for the British and, when asked to subscribe to the act of the Revolutionary Assembly, he refused, fled and was later banished from residing in the United States.

Dr. Haliburton came to Halifax in 1782 and was immediately appointed surgeon to the King's Naval Hospital, which had recently been built on the Halifax side of the harbour near the narrows. Four years later, the Loyalist Claims Commission awarded him 2,500 guineas for his loss of income and expenses, and gave him the option of remaining in Halifax as surgeon to the Naval Hospital or taking charge of the Naval Hospital in New York. Dr. Haliburton chose to remain in Halifax.

During the 1790s Haliburton was in charge of prison hospitals in Dartmouth and on Melville Island, which housed French and Spanish prisoners-of-war. He was appointed to the Council of Twelve in 1787 and served continuously on that governing body until his death in Halifax in 1808. While practicing in Newport, he met and married Susannah, the daughter of Jahleel and Mary Brenton. They had six children, the most well-known being Sir Brenton Haliburton, who served as Chief Justice of Nova Scotia from 1833 to 1860.

— *Allan Marble*

ALFRED SAMUEL HAMSHAW
1914–1993
Buried at Pleasant Hill Cemetery, Lower Sackville

Everyone who knew Alfred Hamshaw called him Alfie and recognized him as a community builder.

Alfie was born to a remarkable woman, Mary Hamshaw, who immigrated to Saskatoon in 1913 with her husband and baby. After Alfie's father was killed in action in World War I, Mary decided to return home to England. But in Halifax, she heard about the difficulties of life in post-war England and remained in the city. After three years, she found a property on Kearney Lake and the family began a new life as pioneers in the beautiful wilderness.

Alfie Hamshaw (standing, right) and friends enjoy a fishing trip, c. 1947.

Alfie and his brother Dennis swam, fished, boated, carried wood and water, fed the animals and helped with the garden. They walked two miles each way to attend a one-room school in Rockingham. On Sundays, the family attended the Rockingham United Church, where Alfie sang in the boys' choir and became choir president.

As a parent, a businessman and a member of a growing community, Alfie helped establish the Masqwa paddling club, the Centennial Rink and the Rockingham Yacht Club. He sat on the Board of School Trustees, and while he was chairman, the Rockingham School grew from two to ten rooms. Later, from 1978 to 1988, he served as an alderman.

Alfie had a reputation for direct action. When Dunbrack Street was under construction amid much debate, the city manager said that Halifax City should study Alfie's choices: "That guy can get trucks, gravel, bulldozers, he can get anyone to work for him for nothing!" When the Fairview community needed its own rink for minor and junior hockey, and the County could not afford to build one, local residents including Alfie formed a fundraising committee. After negotiating with the landowners, Alfie acquired the land for a dollar, and the rink was built.

As the president of Masqwa, Alfie also negotiated for land on Kearney Lake, persuading the Province to donate several acres. Members opened up the roads and created pathways, wharfs and a beach. Alfie found different contractors to donate fill and, instead of constructing a clubhouse, he arranged to have a house relocated to the lake. Although the house cost $5,000 to move, Masqwa rented it for only a dollar.

Alfie, who died in 1993, did not expect thanks for helping to shape the community into a better place. He simply followed his mother's motto: "Do something today to make the world a better place to live in."

— *Sharon Ingalls*

NOA HEINISH
1893-1975
Buried at Shaar Shalom Cemetery, Halifax

Noa Heinish was a kind and charitable person. A large man, he often intimidated people with his booming voice, but children loved to see him coming. He welcomed many refugees and became a well-loved volunteer at Pier 21.

Heinish, who emigrated from Romania in the 1930s, represented the Jewish Immigrant Aid Society in Halifax. Heinish and his wife, Sarah, lost their only son, a rear gunner in the RCAF in World War II, on his first flight over Germany. They soon adopted two children who had survived the

Sarah and Noa Heinish.

Holocaust, and they found a wonderful home.

Heinish ran a successful clothing business on Gottingen Street from 1923 until 1972. It was one of the first in Halifax to allow customers to buy on credit.

He was an active volunteer in a community that was not always open to minority groups. He helped start the Shaar Shalom Synagogue in 1953 and served as its first president. He worked with numerous Jewish groups, chaired the Nova Scotia war efforts committee of the Canadian Jewish Congress and, after the war, helped orphans and displaced persons. He served as treasurer of the Children's Aid Society and co-chaired the Canadian Council of Christians and Jews.

The Foundation Noa and Sarah Heinish was set up and continues to benefit the community today. The Heinish Learning Centre, which is filled with computers, audio visual equipment and books for children and adults, officially opened in 2004 at the Halifax North Memorial Library on Gottingen Street.

— *Marianne Ferguson*

DORIS LIDZ HIRSCH
1926-2003

When Doris Hirsch was practicing psychiatry in the 1950s and 1960s, there were many challenges to her succeeding in her profession. But Hirsch could always rise to the occasion.

She was born on Long Island, New York, in 1926. She was the daughter of one of the wealthy Lidz brothers who made their money manufacturing buttons. It was not long before Doris, extremely bright and energetic, decided to follow her uncle, Dr. Theadore Lidz, a well-known and effective psychiatrist.

Hirsch, then Lidz, became one of 15 women in a class of 75 at the Johns Hopkins School of Medicine. During her residency training at Johns Hopkins, she met a dynamic young man from Nova Scotia; Doris and Sol married, and enriched our belle province when they returned in 1954 to practise psychiatry.

Dr. Hirsch was the sole female physician on staff at the Victoria General Hospital at that time. Considering herself an adult psychiatrist, she demonstrated significant resilience when the reigning department head appointed her a child psychiatrist — most probably because she was the only woman. She took the project on with her usual good humour, not shrinking from the task even when she observed the toys on the child psychiatry unit included a dart board and standard pointed darts.

Dr. Hirsch's many students, including this writer, loved and admired her. We have fond memories of her characteristic and infectious laugh that she exhaled with enthusiasm and a great shrug of the shoulders at times when lesser humans would have yelped in frustration. At a time when distancing patriarchal models still prevailed in psychiatric practice and training, Dr. Hirsch valued the healing power of a caring relationship and became a pioneer in the practice of what has come to be known as Relational Theory.

Although she had to reschedule a number of patients from the delivery room, Dr. Hirsch did not let the absence of maternity leave stop her from bringing three sons into the world. "She was never really old in her mind," said her son David. "She could sit down with her four grandchildren and become a part of their world."

When Doris died at 77 she was still a vibrant and busy member of Dalhousie's Department of Psychiatry.

— Mary Lynch

SARAH HOWARD
1816–1871
Plaque and bust, Founders Square, Hollis Street

The inscription on the plaque at 1701 Hollis Street describes Sarah Howard as "Halifax's foremost Victorian business woman." Next door, on the corner of Hollis and Prince Street, S. Howard and Son sold European-designed fashions to the city's most discerning female shoppers in what is still a beautiful building today.

Howard was a business pioneer and knew how to get things done. Her advertisements in the *Acadian Recorder* were bigger than most, featuring "Mikado and Black Silks," "a charming collection of Parisian millinery," and the $1.25 "Lome Corset, a symmetrical glove-fitting corset made especially for our retail trade." Her four-wheeled delivery carts also carried store promotions and she was one of the first business owners to employ commercial travelers. Her son Henry lived in London, England, and worked as her buyer. She also employed experienced European designers to oversee the millinery, mantle and dressmaking departments of her business.

Sarah Howard Building, 1695 Hollis Street, c. 1913.

The local business establishment applauded her business acumen in 1876 in *Halifax and Its Business*, noting "the handsome freestone building" that opened about 1867, its layout and the modern facilities. They made special mention of the second-floor millinery showroom. "[N]o wonder the daughters of fashion make haste to offer their devotion at this shrine!"

Little is known about how Howard got her start, but after her husband Norman Howard died, she began two small shops on Granville Street. She operated a dressmaking shop herself and, with her son Henry, ran a dry goods store.

After a short illness, Howard died in Boston at the home of her other son, Captain William Howard. Ten years later, S. Howard and Son closed its doors, but the gracious building which she commissioned still remains.

— *Roma Senn*

CATHERINE SUSAN ANN MCNAB HOWE
1806-1890
Buried at the Camp Hill Cemetery, Halifax

Catherine Susan Ann McNab Howe managed *The Nova Scotian* and handled the newspaper's finances while her more famous husband Joseph Howe, the father of responsible government in Nova Scotia and former premier and lieutenant-governor, travelled the province.

Susan, or "Susy Anny" as Joseph affectionately called her, was born in Newfoundland, where her father, Captain John McNab, was stationed during the War of 1812. The family moved to McNab's Island, owned by her uncle, when she was 10. They traveled in high social circles; the Duke of Kent was one of their distinguished guests.

It took the charms of Howe to get Susan off the island, where she had honed her singing and needlework skills. Howe, a notorious ladies' man, used to row to the island to woo her. The McNabs worried about Joe's finances until he bought *The Nova Scotian*, and eventually agreed to the marriage. Susan and Howe were married at St. Paul's Anglican Church even though Susan was raised Presbyterian.

Howe had a son named Edward from a previous relationship, and Susan openly welcomed him. The couple went on to have 10 children of their own, but only five lived to adulthood.

Howe took annual trips around Nova Scotia, which he called "rambles," to spread the word about his newspaper, and left many responsibilities to his wife. She was the managing editor and business administrator when her husband

J.E. Woolford's York Redoubt from the Northwest Arm (c.1818) shows the Howe family home in the foreground.

travelled, earning another nickname from Howe: "Little Editor." Despite Howe's public relations efforts, the newspaper did not make them rich, and it was often up to Susan to deal with the financial pressures.

Although Howe was often away, he sent her many affectionate letters to keep up their spirits. In turn, she sent him shirts, razors, ginger beer, oysters and custard. Susan, who did not share her husband's yearning for social activism, solidly supported him, especially during his libel trial. She continued to live her life quietly, without a desire for drama. When Howe went to the United States as an army recruiter, she wrote: "I do not like what you are engaged in but suppose you are all wiser and I should feel satisfied."

Despite her husband's eventful and successful life, Susan was left a poor widow when Howe died in 1873. She had to depend on her children until the provincial government granted her an annuity in 1885.

With her open-mindedness and journalism, Susan was in many ways ahead of her time.

— *Jennifer Morrison*

JOHN EARDLY WILMOT INGLIS
1814-1862

In the summer of 1857, an obscure British Army officer from Halifax was catapulted onto the world stage, attaining the status of Victorian hero. In May, the Indian Mutiny had broken out, forcing the outnumbered British to withdraw into fortified compounds. At Lucknow, 1,720 soldiers, loyal natives and civilians occupied a 15-hectare complex centred on the Residency, a large stone structure. Command soon devolved upon Lieutenant-Colonel John Eardly Wilmot Inglis of the 32nd Regiment.

Inglis was born in Halifax in 1814. He was the grandson of Charles Inglis, the first Anglican bishop of Nova Scotia. He attended the University of King's College — founded by his grandfather — and joined the 32nd Regiment in 1832, becoming its commanding officer in 1855. Inglis was an uninspiring commander, but he was brave and well served by his subordinates. Like many British officers, Inglis was accompanied to India by his wife, Julia, and their three children. Rarely in wartime have

This portrait of Major General John Inglis in full military dress hangs in the Red Chamber of Province House.

soldiers' families been so close to the fighting.

Inside the compound, defenders succumbed daily to enemy fire, disease and suicide. As the heat rose and rations ran short, rebel firing reduced the garrison' walls to a crumpled ruin and the air soon filled with the pungent odours of the excrement and the dead. On July 20, 1857, the mutineers launched their first attack, which was successfully beaten off with slight British losses. Constant assaults and bombardment continued into the fall, taking a heavy toll on Inglis. He experienced dizziness and headaches, while his hair turned prematurely grey.

Finally on September 25, a 3,200-man relief column fought its way into the wreckage of the Residency. The sorely tried defenders were overjoyed; after 87 days, salvation had arrived. Unfortunately, the sense of relief was short-lived as the reinforcements were insufficient to drive the rebels back. On November 17, another force of over 5,000 men relieved the Residency for a second time after bloody hand-to-hand struggles. The garrison quietly withdrew six nights later; nearly five months of living hell were over.

Inglis was promoted to Major-General and knighted. The Nova Scotia Legislature presented him with a sword of honour and a full-length oil painting was commissioned, which now hangs in Province House. Halifax named Lucknow Street in his honour. Fittingly, it intersects with Inglis street, named after his grandfather. Unfortunately, Inglis did not live long to enjoy life as Major-General Sir John.

While travelling Germany in 1862, Inglis died of a fever, perhaps caused by the strain of Lucknow.

— *John Boileau*

SALTER DOWNING INNES
1899-1953
Buried at Camp Hill Cemetery, Halifax

Salter Downing Innes was a food innovator who came up with the idea for a dish people still love today: the chickenburger. In 1940, Innes's son, Jack, and daughter-in-law, Bernice, opened a canteen in Bedford. With the war on and price restrictions in effect, the price of a menu item couldn't be increased unless it changed in some way. When Jack and Bernice decided that they needed to increase the price of their chicken rolls to 25 cents from five cents, Salter suggested that they put chicken in a hamburger bun and call it a chickenburger. The strategy worked, and in 1951, Jack and Bernice's canteen became Bedford's famous Chickenburger.

Salter Innes started life on his family's 750-acre farm in Porters Lake,

Among his many ventures, Salter Downing Innes (far right) ran a canteen at the Halifax Forum. Photo c.1940.

Nova Scotia, in 1899. He grew up with three brothers and three sisters, a direct descendent of Berowald, the founder of the family in 1160 A.D. In British heraldic tradition, this would allow Innes the title of "Sir." Lord Lyon, the arbiter of heraldry for the British Isles, is also of the Innes family.

Early in life, Innes left for Salem, Massachusetts, likely working in the food business. On his frequent returns home, he saw there were ample opportunities, one being in potato chips. He was the first to manufacture, package and distribute potato chips in Nova Scotia, travelling by truck from Shelburne to Sheet Harbour.

He later managed the Ideal Dairy on Hunter Street, which sold milk, cream, butter and eggs.

In 1929, he started Sunnyside, a canteen that sold hotdogs and hamburgers near the Sackville River at the intersection of Highways 2 and 7 in Bedford. Innes selected the name Sunnyside after seeing it posted on a visit to Coney Island in the United States.

His grandson, Jack Innes, said the place burned down perhaps three times with the fryers frequently turning into fire-belching dragons. But each time, Innes rebuilt the canteen and, with pre-war and wartime activity at the Bedford Rifle Range, Sunnyside prospered. To generate traffic, Innes would invite his friends from Halifax to come out for a burger on a Sunday afternoon.

After the end of World War II, Innes sold Sunnyside and the Riverside Restaurant and Cabins to his son-in-law, Arthur Hustins. The restaurant and cabins were located where the Sunnyside Place office building stands today.

At about this time, Salter started operating the now-closed White Spot restaurants in Yarmouth and the Bright Spot restaurant at Lake Banook in Dartmouth. He also operated canteens on the Halifax waterfront and at the Halifax Forum.

— *Tony Edwards*

ROBERT JAMISON
1808-1884
Buried at St. Stephen's Anglican Church Cemetery, Ship Harbour

Robert Jamison.

With a knapsack on his back and an umbrella that he used as a walking stick or for protection from the frequent rain showers, Reverend Robert Jamison traversed the rugged terrain of his vast parish, which extended from Musquodoboit Harbour to Country Harbour.

He was born in Northern Ireland where he received a sound classical education at the Academical Institution in Belfast. Jamison and his family immigrated to Nova Scotia and settled in Dartmouth. He taught school from 1832 to 1839, and assisted the rector of Christ Church along the parish's Eastern Shore. In August 1840, Jamison took up residence at Ship Harbour but was frequently absent.

To notify the neighbouring inhabitants of an intended service, a beacon fire was lit on a prominent hill in the community where Jamison would conduct the service. Shortly thereafter, a congregation would gather; some people would walk through the tangled forest paths, while others would arrive in fishermen's boats from the adjacent islands.

Travel was indeed difficult but certain parts of his parish contained bridle paths or sleigh roads by the late 1840s. After conducting service in Jeddore one Sunday in 1846, Rev. and Mrs. Jamison returned home in a sleigh via eight miles of ice-covered lakes. Such a mode was treacherous because snow had melted and up to two feet of water lay above the ice in some locations. Occasionally the sleigh was afloat in the water, but they managed to travel six miles without much difficulty. Then suddenly, the horse broke through the ice, leaving the sleigh and passengers sitting over the edge of the chasm. Matilda Jamison suggested the horse be disengaged from the sleigh, which her husband successfully did by removing the harness. They then dragged the sleigh from the horse and away from the vicinity of the hole. None the worse for their experience, the Jamisons and their horse completed the rest of their journey without further problems.

Jamison devoted his entire adult life to education and religion. For many years, he was a school commissioner and president of the School Board for the Shore District. The school in Oyster Pond, which opened in 1957, is named in his honour. Jamison's extensive parish, with only one minister in 1840, was eventually divided into smaller parishes with five Anglican ministers by 1884. Travelers can still see Jamison's legacy of a "line of churches" at Jeddore, Oyster Pond, Ship Harbour and Tangier.

— *Philip Hartling*

JAMES ROBINSON JOHNSTON
1876-1915
Buried in the family plot at Camp Hill Cemetery, Halifax

As many as 10,000 people attended the funeral of James Robinson Johnston. The prime minister of his day was among many who sent telegrams of condolence. Yet shortly after his death, Johnston was largely and intentionally forgotten.

Being a lawyer was the centre of Johnston's life. Ironically, after his death, it was the legal process that severely tarnished his reputation and led to his name being seldom mentioned for 75 years thereafter.

It wasn't until the 1990s —when the prestigious James Robinson Johnston Endowed Chair in Black Canadian Studies and the James Robinson Johnston Graduate Scholarship for African Canadians were established at Dalhousie University — that Johnston was remembered again.

The man who became known as "Lawyer Johnston" to his contemporaries was the first Nova Scotian-born black to graduate from Dalhousie University. He also went on to be the first admitted into the Nova Scotia Barristers' Society as a practicing lawyer. At the time he was only the third Canadian-born black to have become a lawyer in all of Canada. This was an outstanding achievement for the grandson of a refugee slave who entered public school at a time when schools in Halifax were segregated.

Johnston was a very prominent member of Halifax's black community. He became secretary of the African Baptist Association of Nova Scotia, an officer of Cornwallis Street Baptist Church and superintendent of its Sunday school.

Lawyer Johnston's law practice focused principally on criminal and military law, the latter largely defending military personnel in court martials. In his most celebrated case Johnston successfully represented, free-of-charge, an Irish Catholic immigrant charged with murdering his mother-in-law, who had been killed by several sledge hammer blows to the head.

Johnston himself was murdered in his home by his brother-in-law, Harry

James Robinson Johnston was the first African-Nova Scotian to graduate from Dalhousie University's Law School. Photo c.1906.

Allen, who shot him a number of times in the head at close range because Johnston had ill-treated his wife — an unlikely allegation. Allen was convicted of the murder, but his death sentence was commuted.

Immediately after Johnston's death the Nova Scotia Barristers' Society met in a special session and resolved that the members of the Society attend his funeral en masse, a mark of the esteem he had attained in the legal profession.
— *Greg Arsenault*

SIR EDWARD KENNY
1842-1891
Buried at Holy Cross Cemetery, Halifax

After Sir Edward Kenny resigned from the Senate in 1876, it was said humorously that he had done so because "there wasn't enough life there to suit him."

A native of Kilmoyly, County Kerry, Ireland, Kenny and his brother Thomas probably immigrated to Halifax circa 1824 to serve as clerks in the firm of the Irish merchant John Lyons. By 1828, the brothers had established their own dry goods firm, which operated after 1850 from a handsome building they erected on the southwest corner of George and Granville Streets, site of the present-day Dennis Building.

Kenny took an active political role, serving as Mayor of Halifax, president of the Nova Scotian Legislative Council from 1857 to 1867, member of the Canadian Senate and Receiver-General in the first administration of Sir John A. MacDonald.

Kenny supported the campaign for Halifax's status as a city and served as alderman. A promoter of education, he was one of the original trustees of Saint Mary's College, the predecessor of Saint Mary's University. He was President of the Charitable Irish Society of Halifax and, in concert with other Irishmen, contributed to the Irish Repeal Movement and to relief of the suffering resulting from the Great Irish Famine of the late 1840s.

Despite having served in the administration of Sir John A. MacDonald and having been a leader in Reform politics in Nova Scotia, Kenny was on the liberal side of what MacDonald described as the "Liberal-Conservative Party." Joseph Howe's contretemps with the Catholics in the late 1850s resulted in Kenny and many of his co-religionists switching to the Conservative fold. He went to Rome in 1879 to persuade the Vatican that despite its disapproval of liberalism in Europe, "liberal" was not a bad word in Canada and effectively did a service here by getting the church disentangled from undue interference in political life.

Kenny was knighted in 1872. Today, his descendants live in France.

— *Cyril Byrne*

HELEN KENNY
1850-1897
Buried at Holy Cross Cemetery, Halifax

The brilliant, beautiful and talented Helen Kenny, hostess, suffragette and wife of business leader J. F. Kenny, exemplified Halifax in the late nineteenth century when it was called "The Most British Imperial City in the Western Hemisphere."

When a whole city mourns the sudden death of its most celebrated hostess, one starts to realize the impact such a woman had on a city. A young Kenny had been well educated at a convent in Montreal and burst upon Halifax high society in 1875. Said to be the most beautiful woman in Halifax, she astounded everyone, rich and poor, with her ability to rally public support for the rights of the poor, the arts, and most certainly the right for women to vote in Canada.

Kenny's closest dear friend and ally was the renowned Anna Leonowens, former tutor to the Royal Court of Siam. No two women could be more unalike and yet similar in their objectives — especially in supporting the establishment of a major arts school in Halifax and in trying endlessly to convince provincial and municipal male politicians to legalize women's right to vote. They led many campaigns together, with Kenny's grace and charm complementing Leonowens' forceful and often harsh verbal attacks for their cause. They were a social and political force to be reckoned with and, during their popular campaigns, finally achieved several major successes with the opening of Halifax's Victoria School of Art and Design, now the Nova Scotia College of Art and Design, and nearly won the right to vote for women in 1893, which would have been a first in the British Empire.

Kenny founded the Women's Work Exchange and assisted many other charities in Halifax. As a renowned hostess in her magnificent home on Pleasant Street, now Barrington Street, Kenny bewitched the likes of princesses, Oscar Wilde and Rudyard Kipling. Her charm did much to raise Halifax's profile across North America. She had that innate ability to create excitement, enthusiasm and admiration, and did much to improve the calibre of life and style in Victorian Halifax.

— *Allan Doyle*

JOHN BAPTISTE KOPIT
1698-C. 1759
Perhaps buried in an unmarked grave in Point Pleasant Park, Halifax

John Baptiste Kopit, the son of Paul and Cecile Kopit, Chief of a Mi'kmaq tribe in Shubenacadie, defended his country against the designs of a brutal European invader, Great Britain.

Chief Kopit did his best to find peace with the British, as witnessed by the Peace Treaty of 1752, which reaffirmed earlier treaties. It called for an end to hostilities and contained provisions regarding hunting, fishing and trading. But in 1753, two Englishmen committed a horrendous crime that laid the groundwork for the resumption of war. They slaughtered and scalped seven members of a Mi'kmaq family and tried to collect a bounty for the scalps when they brought them to Halifax. The British did not arrest and try the two for murder, as required by the treaty with Kopit, and they walked free. As a result, war again resumed and continued for another eight years.

The Mi'kmaq fondly remember Kopit as a peacemaker and hero, who tried to preserve his nation against impossible odds.

— *Daniel N. Paul*

LESLIE KOVACS
(1921–1993)
&
EDITH KOVACS
(1923–1976)
Both buried in Shaar Shalom Cemetery

Both Les and Edith Kovacs suffered in Nazi concentration camps. A psychiatrist and a family doctor, respectively, they later became well-liked, respected Canadians, who made Dartmouth their home and a welcoming place for many visitors.

Both Edith and Les were born in Hungary but did not meet each other until later in life. Edith grew up comfortably in Polgar, where her mother owned and managed a mill. Les's family had changed the family name from Karpeles to Kovacs to lessen the persecution they faced as Jews. It didn't work. And their lives changed when Hitler captured Hungary.

Edith was sent to Auschwitz, a death camp where millions were murdered. Les wrote about his seven months in a labour camp where he worked hard, receiving two meals a day and five hours of sleep each night.

Edith and Leslie Kovacs.

Les told this story:

> When carrying a heavy log, he dropped it and fell down.
> The guard who was usually "nice" rushed up and started
> beating him with a rifle butt. Finally he stopped, threw the
> rifle on the ground and started sobbing. The guard said he
> had lost his family in an air raid. Les tried to console him,
> handed him his rifle and walked away carrying the log.

Later, the Nazis sent Les on a six-day walk through body and rat-infested fields to Mauthausan, a concentration camp.

After liberation in 1945, Edith suffered tuberculosis (T.B.) and was sent to a sanatorium in Sweden. Following a year-long convalescence, she worked there as a maid for two years.

In 1949, Edith met Les, by then a chest specialist, at a Budapest sanatorium, where she had been readmitted with T.B. Edith later enrolled in nursing at the Jewish hospital in Budapest, attended a boarding school, and completed four years of high school in a single year. She started first-year medicine in 1951.

The couple married in 1953 at noon at Budapest City Hall, returning to work that afternoon. Three years later, the Hungarian Revolution erupted and the family, which now included their baby Katalin, decided to escape the violence. Claiming their daughter needed medical attention, they arranged to visit a hospital near the Austrian border. They travelled by ambulance, and then walked through the woods in the dark to the border. Using false papers, they successfully crossed the Iron Curtain in 1957.

From Austria they travelled to Italy to board a plane for Montreal. Things didn't go according to plan, when they missed their flight while trying to quench Edith's craving for ice cream. Eventually they sailed to Canada via Spanish Morocco on the *Ascania*. They arrived in Saint John, New Brunswick, not speaking any English, with a suitcase, documents and the clothes on their backs.

Eventually Edith, with Les's encouragement, returned to medical school at Dalhousie University and graduated in 1962, while Les specialized in psychiatry. During that time, they had another child, a son named George.

As doctors, they became active community members. Edith, who was warm and gracious, worked at the Nova Scotia Hospital, taking pleasure in helping others. After a diagnosis of leukemia in 1973, she continued to practise medicine despite monthly chemotherapy. She died at the age of 53, with few besides Les knowing her life story.

Les, an avid reader of music, history and art, played the cello and continued to see his patients well past retirement age. He had an open-line policy with patients, letting them call him at any time. Despite all the medical advances he knew his patients sometimes just needed someone who believed in them.

— Leah Kovacs Schweitzer and Hannah Kovacs

ARGYRIS LACAS
1896-1997
Buried at Fairview Cemetery, Halifax

At the time of his death at 100 years old, Argyris Lacas was affectionately known as Papou (grandfather) to most of Halifax's Canadian-Greek community as well as his own family.

Born in 1896 on the Greek Island of Icaria, then under Turkish rule, Lacas left home at 14 to join his older brother in Alexandria, Egypt. Having

Argyris Lacas (far left) participates in a re-enactment of the arrival of a Greek family to the port of Halifax, 1986.

worked there as an electrician, Lacas later moved on to join other family members who had immigrated to the United States. Arriving in 1918 at New York's Ellis Island, he had to remain there for six months because quotas for Greek immigrants in the U.S. were full. Later he worked in Montreal, Philadelphia, and New York, where he met his future wife, Dina Petropolis. Eventually they moved to her home in Halifax, where the couple married and raised a family.

Lacas was a devoted family man who also held a deep affection for the people of the Halifax Greek community. Today, adults from that community recall how Lacas often met them and their parents as they walked on Citadel Hill or in the Public Gardens. Inevitably, Lacas would reach deep into his pockets, pull out some quarters and bestow them on the children for ice cream.

During his working years in Halifax, Lacas helped operate the Cameo Restaurant, opened the Doric Restaurant, worked in the insurance industry and owned a jewellery business. In all those businesses, he made it a point to hire, train and assist Greek immigrants. A founding member of St. George's Greek Orthodox Church in Halifax, Lacas particularly liked helping individuals — whether he could do so by translating for newly arrived immigrants at Pier 21, or simply by taking someone home for dinner. His son-in-law said of him: "My mother-in-law never knew how many people were coming to Sunday dinner because her husband was always bringing someone home with him."

Lacas was the co-founder of the Halifax branch of American Hellenic Educational Progressive Association (AHEPA), an organization that endeavoured to promote education among young Canadian Greeks. After his death in 1997, the Halifax AHEPA established an annual scholarship in his memory.

— *Geraldine Thomas*

HILDA MARY SLAYTER LACON
1882-1965
Buried in the family plot at Camp Hill Cemetery, Halifax

Hilda Mary Slayter Lacon was an upper-middle-class Haligonian who survived both the sinking of the *Titanic* and the Halifax Explosion. Born at 64 Argyle Street in 1882, she was the daughter of Dr. William B. Slayter and Clarissa Underhill Clark, and the tenth of eleven children.

At about four years of age, Lacon sailed with her siblings, mother and servants to Europe. In Germany, the family settled in Bamburg, attended school and lived for several years. All family members were gifted musicians or singers; indeed Hilda hoped for an operatic career.

Hilda went to Italy to study voice, but discovered that her voice was not strong enough to sing professionally. In April 1912, she booked passage for America and was transferred to RMS *Titanic*. She was successful in obtaining a place in lifeboat 12 for herself. Arriving in New York, she was interviewed by the *New York Times*, an interview that was republished in the Halifax newspapers.

Photo of Hilda Slayter Lacon, c.1911.

Travelling to British Columbia, she married Henry Reginald and, on Denman Island, she gave birth to their only child, Reginald. When war broke out in 1914, her husband enlisted and Hilda soon found herself living in Halifax again, first at 6 Brenton Place and later at 153 Pleasant Street.

On December 6, 1917, she endured the Halifax Explosion. Covered in ceiling plaster and soot, she and her son made their way to the residence of the aged Mrs. George W. Francklyn on South Park Street.

In her early years, Lacon met royalty on many occasions. Her earliest recollection was meeting HRH Prince George of Wales in 1890 while he was in command of HMS *Thrust*. As a debutant, Lacon would again meet Prince George on his tour of Canada in 1901. In 1903, her brother was an officer on board the Royal Yacht *Victoria & Albert*; the family was staying at Southsea near Portsmouth. Invited to dinner, she had the opportunity to meet King Edward VII and his nephew, King Alphonso XII of Spain.

In her last years of her life, Lacon visited Halifax. She never mentioned the *Titanic* or the Halifax Explosion during her time there. Rather, her advice to Haligonians was to "save older buildings."

— *Garry D. Shutlak*

SISTER MARGARET LAHEY
1903-1987
Buried at Mount Olivet Cemetery, Halifax

Sister Margaret Lahey could be seen strolling the hallways at the Convent of the Sacred Heart arm in arm with a student, surrounded by a group of others waiting their turn for her attention. She was always there to listen to every girl's story and share her joys and sorrows.

An unforgettable teacher, loyal friend and religious figure, Sister Lahey left an imprint on those fortunate enough to know her during their school years at the 1852-built school on Spring Garden Road, a home and school for the religious order of the Sacred Heart's boarders, students and teachers.

Sister Margaret Lahey (centre) receives flowers from her Grade 8 class on the last day of school in June 1972.

In the 1970s, as the grade seven home-room teacher, Sister Lahey was responsible for students in grades six, seven and eight (known as Lower Seniors), and schooled them in the new wing of the Convent. For many students, this was a new school, with new rules to learn along with the age-old Sacred Heart tradition of the weekly award ceremony, as well as Friday chapel and morning assembly in the study hall. She guided many students through their teenage years with firm direction and gentle persuasion.

As a child, for six years beginning in 1917, she would take the ferry to Halifax to attend the Convent for because Dartmouth had no Catholic schools, and attained a perfect attendance record. She made her novitiate in Kenwood Albany in 1924 and received a Bachelor of Arts degree from Fordham University in New York.

Later as principal of Halifax's College Street School during the Second World War, she faced many challenges. The playground that the school used for baseball or hockey, depending on the season, was expropriated by the military in 1943 for army barracks, causing a public outcry.

After her retirement Sister Lahey volunteered in a literacy program where she continued to touch the lives of students from various ages and education levels. Many remember her as a faithful pen pal, a teacher, a friend, a sister, but most of all, as a mother to all.

— *Sarah Cassidy*

ABBIE LANE
1898-1965
Buried at Camp Hill Cemetery, Halifax

In a career that spanned theatre, journalism and city politics, Abbie Lane is best remembered as an active city councillor who served at a time when few women held public office.

Born in Halifax in 1898, Lane (nee Jacques) and her mother left for Brooklyn, New York, when she was a child. As a young adult, she returned to Nova Scotia to live with her aunt in Truro, receiving a Success Business College certificate and working for the Canadian Bank of Commerce.

For Lane, it was dance and theatre that really inspired her. After returning to Halifax and marrying Fred Lane when she was 26, she joined several local theatrical productions and eventually landed a 20-year stint with CBC Radio's *Gillian Family* serial. She became the first female commentator and

Abbie Lane dances with an unidentified partner in 1958.

later director of research with CJCH Radio as well as serving as women's editor for the *Chronicle-Herald*, a position she reportedly took on a dare.

In addition to her paid duties, Lane was highly committed to charitable organizations such as the Red Cross during World War II, the Halifax Welfare Bureau and the Nova Scotia branch of the Voluntary Registration of Canadian Women, which she chaired. Somehow Lane managed to fit in all her activities while raising three children, to whom she was dedicated. "Somebody has to get those three meals a day and keep the house in good running order," she claimed years later.

Encouraged in 1951 to run as a Halifax alderman, Lane ran a vigorous "kitchen campaign," beating a former mayor two to one to win the post for which she is most remembered. During her career, she implemented an ambitious public housing programme, made recommendations to the provincial minister of health regarding nursing home conditions and represented Canada at a United Nations seminar on the status of women.

Appalled by the lack of female involvement in politics, Lane urged women to become more active to better all fellow humans. She died suddenly in 1965. Halifax's Abbie J. Lane Memorial Hospital is named in this remarkable woman's memory.

— *Hazel Walling*

JOHN PAUL (J.P.) LEBLANC
1921-2002
Buried at Gates of Heaven Cemetery, Lower Sackville

J.P. LeBlanc.

Through his career, tireless volunteer work, and dream of revitalizing Pier 21, John Paul LeBlanc touched the lives of many Canadians.

LeBlanc was born in St. Anselme, New Brunswick, a ninth-generation Canadian. He joined the Air Force and in 1942 headed overseas from Pier 21 — one of 360,000 Canadian military personnel — to serve in World War 11. After 32 missions he returned through Pier 21 with a British war bride, Trudy Tansey, and a desire to continue his spirit of service in civil life. Joining Employment and Immigration Canada, John lived across Canada with his wife in his varied postings, but eventually made Halifax home. He was a past board director with the Canadian Immigration Historical Society. In the seventies, he organized an employment program to help inmates at Dorchester Penitentiary. The inmates, grateful for his help, made him slippers, which he happily wore for years. His dedicated volunteer work for countless groups has often been recognized. The Mi'kmaq chiefs of Nova Scotia presented him with a peace pipe when he retired from government service, and the city of Windsor, Ontario made him an honorary citizen.

In 1988, LeBlanc, a devoted husband and father of five, formed the Pier 21 Society to promote the Pier as a national historic site, and, in time, to create a museum to celebrate both the veterans who passed through Pier 21 and the one million immigrants who were welcomed to Canada at this simple waterfront shed on Halifax Harbour. He called it "the stage upon which unfolded some of the most exciting chapters of 20th-century Canadian history."

On Canada Day, 1999, Pier 21 opened to the public. LeBlanc's dream gave the million-and-a-half individuals whose lives had been touched by Pier 21 a place to remember and to celebrate their lives in Canada.

His literary contributions included co-writing *Pier 21: The Gateway that Changed Canada* and writing *A Portrait of an Acadian Family 1643–1990*. He also contributed articles to *Southender Magazine* and several boating magazines. Remembrances of his wartime service have been donated to the Pier 21 Society.

— *Carrie-Ann Smith*

LIZZIE LEWIS
1873-1952
Buried in Brookside Cemetery, Bedford

Lizzie Lewis ran Bedford's longest-operating guesthouse, which she originally called the "House of Good Service." As the reputation of the house grew, guests arrived from near and far to spend the summer, a week or two, or even just a Sunday dinner.

Lizzie (Elizabeth) was born in 1873 to William and Elizabeth Willis, who came from London and settled in the Bedford area, raising five sons and five daughters. William built two houses but his wife always wanted one with large verandahs, so he started building a third. Unfortunately Elizabeth died before its completion and eventually Lizzie inherited the house.

Lizzie Lewis.

In 1899 Lizzie married Frank Lewis, who operated a farm in the Sackville area. The Lewis House became famous for its farm-fresh eggs, its produce and its wonderful home-cooked meals. Records from the 1930s list room-and-board at $11 a week, and the guest register contains the names of famous people from across Canada. As staunch Presbyterians, the couple maintained rigid rules of conduct: no smoking indoors and guests must arrive for meals on time.

Lizzie was strong-minded and made her views known emphatically. She did not support daylight saving time. The congregation of her church compromised by holding the morning service at 10:30 a.m. standard time. But Lizzie was not impressed, and marched her family into church at 11 o'clock, half an hour late. She strongly opposed church union. When the Bedford Presbyterian Church voted in favour of union in 1925, she withdrew her membership and attended St. David's Presbyterian Church in Halifax, although her husband remained with the Bedford church.

Lizzie encouraged scholastic achievement for her four children. Alice and Frances became professors, and Isabel became assistant superintendent of nursing at a Montreal hospital. Willis (Bill) remained at home to run the farm and business, continuing the excellent service visitors expected. When Frances died in 1978, Lewis House was sold and the contents auctioned off during a mammoth two-day, outdoor event.

The Lewis House is now a private home, but many still remember Lizzie, her boundless energy, her immaculate home and her wonderful cuisine.

— *Marion Christie*

HOW LING
1883-1963
Buried in Mount Pleasant Cemetery, Lower Sackville

In 1900, How Ling arrived in Canada at the age of 17 during a period when the country discouraged Chinese from entering by imposing a head tax. His brother had already settled in New Glasgow, Nova Scotia.

In 1928, Ling arrived in Halifax with his wife, Twe Sing Chong, the second Chinese family to come to Halifax. The couple and their seven children operated a farm in north-end Halifax for 11 years, a difficult time during the Depression. People would often beg for food and vegetables, and, even though they spoke little English, they understood the need and gave generously.

Ling sold his vegetables and meat at the Halifax City Market and was quite a character, wearing coveralls and a wide smile. One Saturday, when he was returning home on the tram car following a visit, his paper bag tore open and live eels slithered across the floor, causing a huge commotion and frightening passengers until he retrieved his dinner.

The Ling farm, which was located on present-day Leeds Street, next to Rockhead Prison and adjacent to Africville, was a haven for many Chinese men, as women were denied entry to the country in those days. They enjoyed family life with the Lings on Sundays. On other days, Ling and his

How Ling and son George, seen here at the family farm on what is now Leeds Street, make their way to the Halifax Farmers' Market. Photo c.1940.

cronies would gamble at the two houses in the city's Chinatown on Grafton and Granville streets. He would often take his savings and head to Montreal for months to gamble.

Although he was a Buddhist and his wife a Catholic, he insisted the family attend church and Sunday school at United Memorial Church on Kaye Street. Reverend Charles Crowdis would warmly welcome the family at church, despite the widespread prejudice against the Chinese in Canada.

Shortly after World War II, Chinese immigrants finally gained the right to vote. On Election Day, Ling would call his daughter for a drive to the polls and proudly and happily cast his ballot, although, with his limited English, he may not have known for whom he was voting. Another proud moment occurred when his three sons, Tom, William and George, found jobs with the federal government, after serving in World War II.

His family went on to create its own United Nations, marrying spouses of Scottish, Norwegian, Chinese, West Indian and Belgian origins.

— Mary Mohammed

WALLACE MACASKILL
1893-1956
&
ELVA MACASKILL
D. 1971
Buried in Gates of Heaven Cemetery, Lower Sackville

Raised in the Bras d'Or Lake region of Cape Breton, Wallace MacAskill spent his boyhood sailing and photographing this shimmering, inland sea. At 16, he travelled to New York to study commercial photography, and was greatly influenced by the art photography of Alfred Stieglitz. He returned to Nova Scotia and worked as a commercial photographer, while also making art photographs of the sea and environs.

He moved to Halifax just before World War I, and photographed events such as the Halifax Explosion. Wallace met and married fellow commercial photographer and Cape Bretoner, Elva Abriel, who shared his love of all things nautical. In 1951, Wallace dedicated a book to Elva, "To my Wife, whose love of the Sea is as great as my own!"

They opened a small shop at 72 Barrington Street, where they made a living — unheard of at that time — selling artistic photographs. Wallace chronicled the dying age of sail and picturesque fishing villages with poetic insight. Elva hand-tinted the photographs, a tradition established by 1850 to enhance a photograph's permanence and illusion of reality. Her pastel haze became their studio's signature. Their business partnership won them international recognition, and the photographs became known simply as "MacAskills."

The couple lived an enviable life in a house called *Brigadoon*, perched on a cliff above Fort York Redoubt, overlooking the approaches to Halifax Harbour. Large, curved windows provided a view of water traffic. At noon, Wallace, a tweedy stocky figure, would ring a brass bell and enjoy his first scotch of the day. The couple sailed their yacht *Highlander*, a sloop of teak and mahogany with a carved thistle on its bow, at every opportunity. Wallace was commodore of the Royal Nova Scotia Yacht Squadron, and won every racing trophy the club offered.

By the 1930s, Wallace had established himself as the world's foremost marine photographer, winning hundreds of awards. He frequently sailed and photographed the *Bluenose*, the unbeatable Lunenburg sailing and fishing schooner. A *Bluenose* stamp was produced based on one of his photographs. Wallace's *Bluenose* also decorates the Canadian ten-cent piece, still in circulation. Three books of his photographs were published, and one was presented to Princess Elizabeth and Prince Philip during their 1951 visit.

Wallace died at *Brigadoon* and Elva sold his glass negatives and the rights to his signature. Some estimate that he took 500,000 art photographs. His photographs continue to be reproduced today, delicately hand-tinted in Elva's palette.

— *Carol Hansen*

CLARA (CLAIRE) P.M. MACINTOSH
1882-1958
Listed in the Book of Remembrance, Nova Scotia Archives

Clara (Claire) MacIntosh could get things done. On December 6, 1917, as Lady Superintendent of the Halifax Central Nursing Division of the St. John Ambulance Brigade, she helped with relief efforts following the Halifax Explosion that devastated the city's north end. In her Robie Street home, she cared for the injured who had come seeking her husband's help and, when forced to evacuate the house, she established a first aid station in the middle

Claire P.M. MacIntosh, c.1950.

of the Commons. Claire organized volunteers to deliver clothing and coal to the destitute, and supervised the work of division members in city hospitals. Writing to Brigade headquarters about their efforts, she said: "I know of cases where they have stayed on duty 20 hours at a stretch and rendered service, which at other times would have been considered impossible."

Clara Pauline Millidge Harris was born in 1882 at Londonderry Mines, Nova Scotia, and attended Edgehill School for Girls. In 1909, she became the first nurse to graduate from the Payzant Memorial Hospital. She worked for the Victorian Order of Nurses before her 1914 marriage to Halifax physician George Arthur MacIntosh, who later served as Superintendent of the Victoria General Hospital. In 1919, Claire bore a son, Ian.

Retiring from the Brigade in 1920, Claire began a 35-year career as author, composer and dramatist. In 1931, as Claire Harris MacIntosh, she published *Attune with Spring in Acadie*, a description in verse and song of the birds of Nova Scotia. This was followed by more songs, poems, plays, children's stories, a pageant and two anthems. She initiated a children's branch of the Theatre Arts Guild called The Young Pretenders, managed the Madame Hylda School of Dramatic Expression and established the Halifax Centre of The British Poetry Society. In 1943, in the joy of receiving a Canadian Drama Association award for her contributions to drama in Canada, she suffered the death of her soldier son, killed while serving in Sicily, Italy.

Moving to Bedford after her husband's death in 1945, Claire continued to write poetry and compose songs while working to memorialize the war sacrifice of Haligonians. In 1950, she was elected the first president of the Halifax County Chapter of the Silver Cross Women of Canada and with members inaugurated the Book of Remembrance. This was presented to the Halifax Memorial Library in 1955, three years before she died.

— *Frances Gregor*

ISABEL MACNEILL
1908-1990
Ashes buried at Camp Hill Cemetery, Halifax

Although women have served continuously in the armed forces since Confederation, Canadian history books fail to reflect that fact. However, Commander Isabel Macneill, the only female commanding officer in all of the Royal Navies during World War II, was a recipient of the Order of the British Empire. She inspired the phrase "A Woman's Place is in Command."

Born in Halifax, Macneill attended Mount Saint Vincent Academy, Nova Scotia College of Art and Design and Heatherley's of London. She later received honorary degrees from Dalhousie and Queen's University.

As Commanding Officer of HMCS *Conestoga*, she led the Women's Royal Canadian Naval Service (WRENS). Later, in an address to Queen's University she noted: "There is a tide in the affairs of women and men that has been sweeping over the barriers which have protected male prerogatives, eroding the traditional differences which once nicely defined the gender roles."

After the Navy, she became the superintendent of the Ontario Training School for Girls, helping transform the institution from a jail to a school, and supporting treatment rather than punishment for troubled children.

When appointed warden of the federal Prison for Women in 1960, Macneill was appalled by the building's physical structure, which appeared more suitably designed for wild animals than for people. She was the first person to separate first-time offenders from more hardened inmates.

About 70 per cent of the women in the Kingston, Ontario, facility were incarcerated for narcotics offences without treatment programs available to them. With assistance from the Elizabeth Fry Society, Macneill started rehabilitation and education programs with psychiatrists, psychologists, social workers and nurses working as a team. Together they pioneered the idea of gradual release for inmates. Some inmates worked in what she considered mind-numbing employment. Since most of these women were intelligent, she was able to institute programs of higher learning and employment within the community, which would later facilitate their assimilation back into society.

Isabel Macneill had not planned to spend most of her working life managing correctional institutions. She began her career as a scenic designer in professional theatre. But as a woman of great strength and compassion, she became a zealous advocate for post-war reform and a champion of individual identity.

— *Roxanne Rees*

ABBÉ PIERRE-ANTOINE SIMON MAILLARD

1710-1762
Buried at the Old Burying Grounds, Halifax

After encouraging the Mi'kmaq to resist the British, Pierre-Antoine Simon Maillard helped the two sides sign a peace agreement. He became "one of the best ambassadors of the French cause in America in the eighteenth century."

Abbé Maillard was born in France and received ecclesiastical training in Paris. His superiors, noting his "zeal and piety," chose him for the Mi'kmaq missions in what is now Cape Breton. Gifted with a flair for languages, Abbé Maillard studied the Mi'kmaq language with another priest in Louisbourg and improved a system of hieroglyphics so the indigenous people could more easily learn Roman Catholic prayers. Abbé Maillard was called "a naturalized Indian as regards language," and officials called on him to train officers as interpreters. He was an exceptional man who played an important role in Ile Royale and Acadia during the last years of the French regime.

Following the Fall of Louisburg, Abbé Maillard pressed the Mi'kmaq to raid against the British but became a prisoner himself, and was banished to Boston and then France. Returning to Nova Scotia with Duc d'Anville, commander of the French armada, he joined the political fray.

After he accepted British peace conditions, a French governor accused him of treason. But his acceptance of the new political reality was driven by his concern for the fate of the Acadians, the Mi'kmaq and the missionaries.

Abbé Maillard came to Halifax around 1760 and became a well-liked British government agent with a salary of £150 and responsibilities to the Mi'kmaq. This was a remarkable achievement during a period when Catholics were barred from holding public office and the French were considered the enemy. When Abbé Maillard died in 1762, there was no consecrated ground other than St. Paul's Cemetery, and Lieutenant-Governor Jonathan Belcher ordered his burial there. It was an almost unbelievable concession at that time.

A plaque on St. Mary's Basilica in Halifax lists Abbé Maillard's many accomplishments. Among them, he performed the first mass, opened the first Catholic Church in Halifax in 1759, and performed services for the Acadians at a Halifax battery to become the "spiritual leader of all dispersed Acadians." He successfully persuaded the Mi'kmaq chiefs to sign peace treaties with the British. As a result of the signing, wrote a settler, "many Englishmen were saved from being massacred."

— *Roma Senn*

JOSHUA MAUGER
C. 1712-1788

Joshua Mauger, who amassed a modest fortune as a merchant in Halifax in the 1750s, aroused strong feelings in his contemporaries. John Salusbury, a British official here at the same time as Mauger, once referred to Mauger as "a proud troublesome sorry Rascal." Governor Cornwallis disliked Mauger, and complained bitterly about him. But Charles Lawrence, Governor from 1756 to 1760, referred to Mauger as "our well beloved Joshua Mauger."

A view of Mauger's Beach Light, painted by artist Lewis Smith.

Mauger came to Halifax shortly after its founding in 1749. Not much is known about his early life. It is known that he was born on the Channel Island of Jersey around 1712, and went to Louisbourg during the English occupation between 1745 and 1749. Mauger's Nova Scotian interests included a rum distillery, numerous ships and extensive property holdings. Mauger also outfitted privateering vessels during the Seven Years' War, 1756–1763.

In 1760, Mauger returned to Britain but retained many of his investments in Nova Scotia and safeguarded them obsessively. His distillery's profitability depended on government protection, and Mauger ensured that duties were low on the molasses the distillery needed and high on imported rum. Mauger and his friends managed to remove from office several governors who tried to change the duties to produce more revenue for the government.

Mauger was well off, but was not as rich as some people have assumed. Like many ship owners then, Mauger lost a number of ships. On one occasion, a group of his own crewmen stole one of his vessels. Another time, Mauger had to pay for the loss of another merchant's ship when Mauger failed to get it insured. Yet another of his privateering ventures turned sour when Mauger's crew was accused of torturing the crew of a captured vessel.

On returning to England, Mauger purchased a country estate and became a Member of Parliament. His life was not easy. He once lamented that he had been a slave to business all his life. His daughter died in the early 1770s. His grief-stricken wife seldom left her bedroom over the next few years before she passed away. Mauger himself was in poor health for a decade or more before his death in 1788.

The only reminder of Mauger in Canada today is the beach named after him on MacNab's Island in Nova Scotia, and Maugerville in New Brunswick. Both were named for him by residents who were grateful for a service Mauger did them.

— Don Chard

ROBERT McCALL
1958-1991
Member of the Nova Scotia Sport Hall of Fame

As an athletic youth who grew up in Dartmouth, Rob McCall competed in track, played tennis and golf, paddled the Dartmouth lakes in summer and skated them in winter. At the age of 12 he began to skate competitively at the Halifax Skating Club, first teaming up with Marie McNeil. By the 1980s, he was one of the best. He won eight consecutive Canadian titles in ice dance and three world bronze medals. Finally, in 1988, he and partner Tracy Wilson from Burnaby, British Columbia, won Olympic bronze.

The saucy, energetic dance pair turned professional and toured for two years with Stars On Ice. McCall also created choreography with Brian Orser, the two-time Olympic silver medallist and a friend since childhood. McCall and Wilson tackled a range of programs unequalled by their peers, won the 1990 World Professional Championships, and appeared to be unstoppable in a sport controversial for more than its hierarchical system.

The news media had begun to report the untimely deaths of young gay men in their prime from complications related to AIDS. Ice-skating, a sport full of emotion, intrigue and the vitality of youth, was losing its male dancers to the disease at an alarming rate.

McCall was able to keep his sense of humour despite his rapid and shocking decline. When the Canadian Figure Skating Association prematurely announced his death on the radio he called in and said, "This is Rob McCall. Rumours of my death are highly exaggerated." He was the first of four of Canada's most prominent dancers to die. By 1992, at least 40 male skaters and coaches from Canada and the United States had succumbed, infected at

Robert McCall and Tracy Wilson were Canada's best dance team in the 1980s.

a time when little was understood about transmission and prevention.

Wilson, who never skated with a partner again, went on to work as an announcer with CBS. She said that skating without McCall was a lonely experience. She and many of McCall's friends skated at an AIDS benefit in McCall's memory called Skate the Dream in Toronto a year after his death. McCall was inducted to the Canadian Skate Hall of Fame in 2003.

— *Carol Hansen*

ADA MCCALLUM
1909-1986
Buried at Pleasant Hill Cemetery, Lower Sackville

When Ada McCallum died in 1986, The Globe and Mail headline read: "Woman a Halifax Legend in Four Decades as Madam." Even kids in neighbouring New Brunswick had heard of Ada. She was the city's "greatest tourist attraction," Doug Harkness told the *Halifax Daily News*.

During World War II, the white-booted "Ada's girls" serviced the servicemen and were known in Russia and Japan. Although she was always discreet and never gave interviews, Robert Linke in *Cities* noted in 1989 that a Canadian publication included "Ada's" on its to-do list in Halifax. Without specifying what Ada did, it said: "Just ask any cab driver."

Details on Ada's life are sketchy. It is believed she grew up on a farm in Manitoba. Court records from 1942 show her convicted as "an inmate in a bawdy house," in what is now Thunder Bay, Ontario. Apparently, she married and divorced three times, and became a single mother in Halifax. She worked out of various locations, including Hollis Street across from Government House.

As many as 30 girls worked for Ada "on a rotating circuit" that included operations in Montreal and Boston. Rumours circulated that she was connected with organized crime. She faced five prostitution-related convictions from 1952 to 1982, and in 1983 was convicted of tax evasion on an income estimated at $3 million. She paid an $18,000 fine.

In a one-hour television documentary, *Madam Ada: More Class than Flash*, Halifax filmmaker Lulu Keating portrayed her as a shrewd businesswoman with clients that included the cream of Halifax society. But Keating found it tough to get anyone to talk and only about 20 people attended Ada's funeral. Her lawyer Ian Palmeter said, "I had enormous respect for her as a person. She was a perfect lady."

— *Roma Senn*

AILEEN MEAGHER
1910-1987
Buried at Mount Olivet Cemetery, Halifax

After a late start in her running career, Aileen Meagher quickly sprinted to the top.

Meagher was born in 1910 in Halifax, and began her running career at Dalhousie University. She had talent and worked hard. By 1930, Aileen was the Canadian record holder for the 100- and 220-yard events, and a member of the Canadian contingent at the 1932 Olympics. She was part of Canada's gold medal British Empire Games women's relay team. Meagher was the worthy recipient of two prestigious awards in 1935. She received the Velma Springstead Trophy as the Most Outstanding Canadian Female Athlete, and the Norton H. Crom Award as the Most Outstanding Canadian Athlete.

Meagher continued to compete in fine fashion. She ran in the 1936 Olympics in Berlin, and won a bronze medal in the 400-yard relay. Two years

This 1951 painting, Brunswick and Buckingham, *shows a nostalgia for the old city of Halifax.*

later, Meagher attended the British Empire Games in Sydney, Australia, winning a silver medal in the 440-yard relay, and a bronze medal in the 660-yard relay. She used her return fare to purchase a round-the-world trip home, travelling from December until May 1939. Travelling was one of the major motivating factors for Meagher to keep up her running career.

After graduating from Dalhousie University, she became a schoolteacher, but kept up her career as a runner. Training for women, however, was not always easy in the thirties as society felt women were too delicate to compete, and there were moves to ban women from participating in the Olympics.

This did not discourage Meagher. Part of her training schedule involved running from her home to school, earning her the moniker "The Flying Schoolmarm." Although many people considered running unacceptable for a female, let alone for a schoolteacher, Meagher took it all in stride: "I had the choice of spending seven cents on the tramway or seven cents for a couple of doughnuts. So I'd run and have the doughnuts."

After retiring from running, Meagher became a full-time teacher, took up painting and became an accomplished artist. Her paintings are in the collections of the Art Gallery of Nova Scotia, Dalhousie Art Gallery, St. Mary's

University Art Gallery, and the Nova Scotia Art Bank.

One of Nova Scotia's top athletes, Meagher was one of the original members of the Nova Scotia Sport Hall of Fame and a member of Canada's Sports Hall of Fame.

Since 1992, runners have competed in the annual Aileen Meagher International Track Classic in Halifax.

— Stephen Coutts

MARIA MORRIS MILLER
1810-1875
Buried at Camp Hill Cemetery, Halifax

Maria Morris Miller, the "Audubon of Nova Scotian field flowers," was the first Nova Scotian woman to gain recognition as a professional artist.

Born in Country Harbour, Guysborough County, she was the daughter of merchant Guy Morris and Sybella (Leggett) Morris. After the death of her father in 1813, her mother moved the family to Halifax, where they travelled in literary and artistic circles. Maria was given art lessons from professional artist W.Y. Jones. By 1830, Maria was teaching art in a school run by her mother, and in 1833 she opened her own drawing school where she taught "fine art in all its branches."

In 1834, Maria began the first of three series of watercolour illustrations of Nova Scotia wildflowers, published as coloured lithographs in 1840, 1853, 1866 and 1867. That year her work was shown as part of the Nova Scotia exhibit at the International Exposition in Paris. For the initial series, Titus Smith, the first scientist to catalogue the flora and fauna of Nova Scotia, brought her live plant specimens and wrote the botanical notes that accompanied the illustrations.

Her work was very well received in the local press. In January 1837, a columnist for the *Novascotian* suggested that "the possession of Maria Morris's botanical illustrations would establish a family's reputation for good taste in art and appreciation of science." In 1840, the *Times* commented that "[e]very wealthy family in the Province should send Miss Maria Morris an order. The boudoir or the drawing room should claim her volume as its most appropriate ornament; aye, although all the vases, petrified dogs, shell boxes, *et hoc genus omne*, which now cumber the round tables were swept into the fire to make room for it."

In 1840, at the age of 26, Maria married 35-year-old Garret Trafalgar Nelson Miller, a wealthy merchant and real estate developer in Halifax. According to family lore, lustre was added to the couple's wedding at St.

Paul's Church by the fact that Maria's dress was made of fabric given to her by Queen Victoria as a token of her admiration for Maria's wildflower illustrations.

For the next decade, the couple lived in LaHave, Lunenburg County, where their three sons and two daughters were born. In the early 1850s, Maria returned to Halifax and to the public eye when she once again advertised her services as a drawing teacher and artist.

Today a substantial collection of her work is held by the Nova Scotia Museum on Summer Street.

— *Janet Guildford*

MOLLY MOORE
1909-1998
Cremated in Halifax

Molly Moore truly knew the value of a dollar. Moore, a quiet philanthropist of modest wealth, was born in Andover, Germany. She started The Molly Appeal to raise money for the Dalhousie Medical Research Foundation, with a $5 donation.

In 1980, a group of Halifax doctors and businesspeople were trying to establish the Dalhousie Medical Research Foundation (DMRF). According to Jean Sloan, the current executive director of the DMRF, Moore was working as a domestic in a house where the founders once happened to meet. Moore heard their discussions, and was truly taken by the need for medical research. As the founders were leaving the house, she approached them to make her donation.

She said she thought that if every Maritimer gave just a dollar, then it would make a real difference. The founders were so touched by her actions that they decided to name their annual public fundraising appeal after her. Moore agreed to be the namesake only if they didn't reveal her identity.

In 1994, Moore allowed the foundation to give her their Outstanding Service Award. She was finally introduced to the public as the founder of the Molly Appeal. At that time, she was a resident in Northwood Manor, a senior's home in Halifax. Jean Sloan would periodically visit Moore, who would have her palms overloaded with change received as donations from the other residents. She didn't like to ask for money, but the residents were inspired by her to give.

Moore lived until the age of 89. In her lifetime, she had seen the program raise almost $4 million through public donations. Each year, every dollar raised through the programme is used to support one of the Dalhousie medical school's four areas of research: neuroscience, cardiovascular research, infectious diseases and immunology, and cancer research. Money from the Molly Appeal is used to leverage further government funding and has gone to support facilities like the Brain Repair Centre and the Core Facility for Experimental Heart Disease.

So just like Molly Moore's original $5 donation, all donations to the Molly Appeal inspire good beyond their face value.

— Ainslie MacLellan

SISTER MARY EVARISTUS MORAN
1870-1953

From her earliest days, founder and first President of Mount Saint Vincent University Sister Mary Evaristus loved to learn.

Mary Elizabeth (Mamie) Moran was born in Roxbury, Massachusetts, in 1870, the fourth child of devout Catholic parents from Northern Ireland. An intelligent and conscientious student, she attended public schools in Roxbury. In her late teens, she met Sister Mary Bonaventure of Charity of Halifax, who had come to Roxbury to open an elementary Catholic parochial school. Sister Bonaventure led Mamie to embrace religious life as a Sister of Charity. In 1889, Mamie sailed from Boston to Halifax to embark on her new life and become known as Sister Mary Evaristus.

She pronounced her vows three years later and began teaching at St. Patrick's in Halifax, back then a school for girls. She spent nearly 25 years there and gained a reputation for her consistent zeal for good education and the integrity of her religious spirit. She understood her students' personal problems, especially those who had to drop out. She often visited their homes and convinced reluctant parents to allow their daughters to continue their education. It began her lifelong commitment to the higher education of women.

At the same time, she furthered her own education. After receiving a Bachelor of Education from the overseas programme at London University, she received a Master's in Latin in 1915 from Dalhousie University. That same summer she began her studies at the Catholic University in Washington, D. C., where she obtained a doctoral degree in Greek literature.

Taking up residence at Mount Saint Vincent Motherhouse, she supervised the sisters' studies to prepare them for the day when the teaching profession would require higher qualifications. She expanded the normal school training, and then worked on facilitating a relationship with Dalhousie University to allow the sisters to study for a degree there. She persuaded teaching sisters from across Canada and the United States to begin private studies. As early as 1925, many sisters had obtained either doctoral or master's degrees, qualifying them to teach at a university.

After discussions with Dalhousie University, a petition to establish Mount Saint Vincent as a separate college was submitted to the Nova Scotia government. Despite strong opposition, Mount Saint Vincent College was established in 1925, and became the first women's college in Canada with the power to grant degrees in Arts and Secretarial Science. Sister Mary Evaristus has always been recognized as the college's founder.

— Sister Marie Gillan

FREDERICK WILLIAM MORRIS
1801-1867
Buried at Camp Hill Cemetery, Halifax

Frederick William Morris was born in Halifax in 1801, the son of Charles Morris and Charlotte Pernette. He attended King's College in Windsor and, after serving an apprenticeship with Dr. William B. Almon, he entered the Faculty of Medicine at the University of Edinburgh in 1821. He graduated with his M.D. in 1825. While at University he invented a surgical saw, which was described in the *Edinburgh Observer*. Returning to Nova Scotia, he practiced briefly in Lunenburg and Annapolis Royal before establishing a permanent practice and a drug store on Hollis Street in Halifax in 1834.

All through his career, Dr. Morris experimented with new medications and wrote articles for medical journals. His pamphlet entitled *Remarks on Spasmodic Cholera* was published in 1832 in which he described how to protect against and treat cholera. In 1833, he advertised his own "Anglers Defence", a mosquito remedy, while in 1838 he advertised "Morris's Peptic Pills", a cure for dyspepsia. In 1839, he advertised that he was giving a course in Chemistry at Dalhousie College, and in 1840 was one of several physicians and surgeons who petitioned the government to establish a hospital in Halifax. In 1855, when the Halifax Dispensary was established on Argyle Street, Dr. Morris was appointed the resident physician and continued in that position until his death in 1867. He came very close to losing this job, however, in 1861 over his involvement in the smallpox remedy affair.

He publicly extolled the merits of a smallpox cure suggested to him by the mysterious "Professor" John Thomas Lane, an Irishman who had been granted the status of a Chief by the Mi'kmaq at Shubenacadie. Dr. Morris stated that he had administered Lane's smallpox cure, which contained the root of the pitcher plant, to several people suffering from smallpox and "it proved remarkably efficacious." The Medical Society of Nova Scotia reacted immediately and supported the motion of Dr. Daniel M. Parker that Dr. Morris's name be stricken from the membership "for being in collusion with a noted empiric." The Board of the Halifax Dispensary met and reprimanded Dr. Morris, but decided to continue his employment as Resident Physician on the condition that he refrain from endorsing medicines prepared by empirics and quacks.

— *Allan Marble*

REAR ADMIRAL LEONARD MURRAY
1896-1971
Ashes spread in a Naval Vault, St. Paul's Church, Halifax

Rear Admiral Leonard Murray became the scapegoat for the infamous Halifax Victory in Europe (VE) Day riots of May 1945. Someone had to take the blame for the two days of mayhem and looting in downtown Halifax following the announcement that World War II had ended.

Rear Admiral L.W. Murray.

A native of Pictou County, Nova Scotia, Murray joined the newly formed Halifax Royal Naval College at the tender age of 15. The Navy was his life and, like most who rise to senior rank, he had a dogged dedication to his profession. As the principal architect and organizer of the Allies North Atlantic Convoy System during World War II, he was the only Canadian to have ever commanded a theatre of war. The Battle of the Atlantic was a major conflict as German U-boats attacked the convoys transporting troops and supplies to Europe. To say the least, Murray had his hands full.

Halifax was poorly equipped to handle the massive influx of military personnel, workers and families who arrived to help with the war effort. In addition, Ottawa failed miserably to ease the burden of Halifax's housing crisis. As a result, merchants and landlords shamelessly gouged the new arrivals. With few places to go and little to drink, supply and demand spurred on the seedy underbelly of Halifax's commerce in prostitution and bootlegging.

Harry MacKeen, a lawyer and a federal Tory candidate, blamed the "insane" liquor laws for the Halifax riots; he had maintained that the situation was ripe for disaster since the church wardens of Fort Massey and the temperance ladies conspired to shut down the AJAX Club, some three years earlier. The AJAX club had provided a valuable meeting place for the displaced and often lonely service members. They could have a meal, a strictly controlled number of drinks and conversation. The closure of this well-run service club left them with no place to socialize.

While the city leaders, including a new mayor with no prior political experience, made celebration plans for VE Day, they neglected to ask service people what they wanted. If anything, it appeared the citizens of Halifax would happily have excluded military personnel entirely from their VE Day celebrations. The mistrust between the military and civilian communities of Halifax climaxed on the day of celebration when Arthur Mahon, the head of the Nova Scotia Liquor Commission, decided to close all the liquor stores without informing the public.

Justice Kellock's Royal Commission and a simultaneous Naval Board of Inquiry convened to investigate how Rear Admiral Murray had conducted his Command. What better way to obtain federal government funds for the expensive cleanup of Halifax than to lay blame at the feet of Halifax's most senior military representative?

Murray resigned, likely at the behest of his wife Jean, and they left Canada for England. Perhaps as a result of the Kellock Commission, Murray embarked on a second distinguished career in law.

— *Roxanne Rees*

JOE NORRIS
1924-1966
Star of the Sea Roman Catholic Cemetery, Terence Bay

Nova Scotian folk artist Joe Norris created art that has only recently gained legitimacy as an art form. His work celebrates the heritage of the ordinary person.

Norris was born in Halifax, one of eight children. His father died when he was seven, and his family moved to Lower Prospect where he grew up in poverty. He rarely attended school because he suffered from pleurisy. Breathing caused him severe pain, and the condition hindered him throughout his life. To keep busy, he began painting as a hobby.

A bachelor, Norris fished and worked in construction until a heart attack at the age of 49 prevented him from working. With more free time, he turned to painting again. He painted canvases, wooden chests, mantles and chairs— decorative objects for everyday living — with charm, simplicity and honesty. His subjects included the seasons, fishing and farming villages, coastal scenes and boats of all sorts. His art dealer, John Houston, noted that Norris was a serious and busy artist, but he always had time for family and visitors, including village kids, stray cats and, oddly, a duck.

He was a man of few words. When journalists such as Peter Gzowski and art dealers wanted Norris to comment on his own work, Norris would reply: "I put it all in the paintings. I just paint." Houston described Norris's paintings as "one man's idea of what heaven might be; a wondrous place where people and the animals share nature in peace and harmony."

The Art Gallery of Nova Scotia exhibited *Joe Norris: Painted Visions of Nova Scotia* from 1973 until 1996 to celebrate the lively spirit of this Nova Scotian folk artist. The exhibition provided a sampling of 200 pieces of Norris's work, demonstrating his vitality and imagination.

— *Bernard Riordon*

ELIZABETH STYRING NUTT
1870-1946

The surviving image in Halifax of Elizabeth Styring Nutt is that of a frumpy old woman in a funny hat holding a painting. Before Nutt arrived in Halifax, however, she had been a friend and associate of Sylvia Pankhurst, the more radical of Emmeline Pankhurst's suffragette daughters, so the familiar image should be superimposed on that of a young woman dressed in the suffrage livery of white, purple, and green and chained to a lamppost in support of votes for women!

Nutt was born on the Isle of Man in 1870 and began her studies at the Sheffield School of Art. She continued under Stanhope Forbes and his Canadian wife, Elizabeth Armstrong Forbes, at their Newlyn school in 1899, and pursued further studies in London, Florence, and Paris. After her thesis on the teaching of colour was published, she returned to Sheffield to teach and exhibit, and had established a reputation at the vanguard of art education reform in Britain in 1919 when she was invited by Arthur Lismer to replace him as principal of the Victoria School of Art and Design in Halifax. In 1925, she changed the name of the school to the Nova Scotia College of Art and began campaigning for a new building.

Self-portrait of Elizabeth Styring Nutt, 1910.

For two decades she devoted herself to the furthering of art in Nova Scotia, and exhibited her own paintings throughout Canada, Britain, France and the United States. With Halifax artists Lewis and Edith Smith, Nutt organized an Art Week in 1922, the success of which led to the founding of the Nova Scotia Society of Artists the following year and the establishment of annual professional art exhibitions in the city. She practised a strain of British Impressionism, already introduced to Nova Scotians by Arthur Lismer, employing vertical strokes with a broad brush in contrast to the generally horizontal strokes of Monet and the French Impressionists.

Her inclusion of a human presence in most of her paintings and her willingness to tackle urban modernism in the 1930s set her apart from the prevailing wilderness mystique of the Group of Seven and reflect her continuing indebtedness to the Impressionists.

The artist failed to get a new art school building with a fireproof exhibition space for the city, but she would, no doubt, be pleased with the City of Halifax Gallery in Honour of Elizabeth Styring Nutt, established at the new Art Gallery of Nova Scotia in 1989 as a permanent memorial to her efforts.

— *Mora Dianne O'Neill*

JOHN O'BRIEN
1831-1891
Buried at Holy Cross Cemetery, Halifax

John O'Brien was the pre-eminent marine artist in the history of Halifax. Born at sea and reared in Halifax within sight of the harbour, O'Brien would seem naturally fit for a career as a marine painter and ship portraitist.

O'Brien may have learned basic painting techniques from John Stevenet Clow, an artist and daguerreotypist active throughout the Maritime region

John O'Brien's Halifax Harbour at Sunset.

since the early 1830s. He may also have taught himself by studying paintings exhibited by traveling dealers in the city.

The artist drew the attention of Haligonians on November 4, 1850, when the *Novascotian* noted that "[y]oung O'Brien, celebrated as a marine painter, took a very creditable sketch of the Flag Ship and Squadron as they went out of harbour on Tuesday last, which he has presented to FW Passow, Esq." (Possibly it was Passow who commissioned the large painting of the subject now in the collection of the Nova Scotia College of Art and Design University.) Before the month was out, the *Novascotian* editor was commending O'Brien's "very creditable sketch in oil colours, of the Race between Mosely's sloop *Mystery*, the Telegraph schooner yacht *Wanderer* and the *Wellington*, a painting now at the National Gallery of Canada.

Commissions from ships' owners and masters kept the young artist busy for several years. The goodwill and financial donations of several of these clients permitted him to receive further training in England in 1857. O'Brien studied in London with marine painter John Wilson Carmichael and attended lectures at the Royal Academy School. Perhaps conscious of the precarious nature of a career in art, O'Brien also used his London sojourn as an opportunity to take lessons in colouring photographs and, after his return to Halifax, worked for Wellington Chase, whose Halifax studio had begun to produce daguerreotypes, ambrotypes and talbotypes in 1857.

Daguerreotype images were developed with mercury fumes. These fumes may have caused the partial blindness that sent O'Brien to Boston for treatment in 1860 and limited his output of paintings thereafter.

O'Brien followed no formula: he painted his ships against white clouds flying through romantic skies, on dramatic storm–tossed seas, or with sails clewed up as they approached the harbour. Throughout his life, he painted Halifax Harbour. Among his early paintings is the 1853 view of the harbour dominated by a Royal Navy frigate and a merchant brig that adorned the cover of Thomas Raddall's *Halifax: Warden of the North*; his final painting was another view of the harbour in which steamships and pleasure craft had replaced the tall ships of his dreams.

— *Mora Dianne O'Neill*

SUSANNAH OLAND
1818-1885
Buried at Christ Church, Dartmouth

In the first year of Confederation, Susannah Oland made a "solitary batch of brown October ale" in her backyard in Dartmouth. Her family and friends liked the beer, and the sixth generation of Susannah's family continues to brew it today in the Maritimes.

An advertisement for the Army & Navy Brewery, c.1870.

The family had come from England in the mid-1860s to help organize the Inter-Colonial Railway, but when that job ended, Susannah and her husband, John, an unemployed accountant, began to sell beer.

With financing from a family friend and an aide to the governor, they began the Army and Navy Brewery to make ale for the military. They bought land in north Dartmouth in what was then called Turtle Grove, a settlement where a group of Mi'kmaq lived until the Halifax Explosion destroyed it and the brewery.

The brewery thrived for several years until John died tragically in a riding accident. Susannah, left with seven children to support, continued on courageously, renaming the brewery S. Oland Sons & Company. It wasn't easy. A fire devastated the brewery in 1878, and Susannah didn't live to see the effects of the Explosion.

Susannah was not a typical nineteenth-century woman, but "a spectacular exception to the rule that barred women from business, trade, and the professions," writes Harry Bruce in *An Illustrated History of Nova Scotia*.

In 1993, Susannah Oland was posthumously inducted into the Nova Scotia Business Hall of Fame.

— *Roma Senn*

WILLIAM PEARLY OLIVER
1912-1989
Buried at Oakridge Memory Gardens, Lower Sackville

William P. Oliver, c.1955.

William Pearly Oliver, who was born in Wolfville, became the minister of the Cornwallis Street Baptist Church in Halifax in 1937, a position he occupied for the next 25 years. As the pastor of the leading black church in Nova Scotia, it was a whole new experience for Rev. Oliver. At Acadia University in Wolfville, he was usually the only black person in a predominantly white environment.

He attended the local high school before graduating from university in 1934 with a Bachelor of Arts and, in 1936, with a Bachelor of Divinity. Several generations of Rev. Oliver's family, who have lived in the province for more than 175 years, attended Acadia. As well, he was a cub master, a scoutmaster and a track star. During World War II, he served as a chaplain in the army.

In Halifax, the other clergy of the community treated him as less than equal. He was treated as a black minister of a black church and not equally entitled. A white lady refused to sell him a home in Windsor, and he was often subjected to such indignities. His church had limited funds and black people were denied access to many occupations to which they were qualified. He viewed such treatment as personal challenges that he tackled, speaking about the equality of man whenever he had the opportunity. He sought the assistance of successful white people to create access for blacks to get better jobs, and he challenged all blacks and whites to contribute money to the church for its repairs and to build a church hall.

He developed organizations such as the Black United Front and the Nova Scotia Association for the Advancement of Coloured People, to educate, encourage and assist black men and women to strive for a better life. A more monumental task was to develop adult education programs to help school dropouts learn to read and write.

This man's success was due in large measure to the unfailing encouragement and support that he received from his faithful, loving and intelligent wife of more than 50 years. Pearline Oliver took care of the upbringing of their five sons, managed women and children's programmes in the church, and stood by her husband whenever he was challenged, insulted or criticized.

Both Oliver and his wife received honorary doctorate degrees and Oliver was invested with the Order of Canada. Their lives have been well documented and make stimulating reading for people concerned with the continuing problems and challenges facing black people in this province and country.

— *Gus Wedderburn*

JOHANNA OOSTERVELD
1943-1994
Cremated in Halifax

Johanna Oosterveld worked tirelessly with unions, dealt with housing, social justice and health issues, and gave a voice to those who lacked the confidence to speak for themselves in an often unjust world.

Born in Holland, she arrived in Halifax in 1971, and applied for a job with a coalition of citizens' groups at the Movement for Citizens Voice and Action (MOVE), a Trudeau-era organization, which deemed her too employable for the job. However, the job needed someone with vision and MOVE soon called her back.

Oosterveld listened, encouraged and celebrated people for independent thought. The citizens' groups in MOVE were diverse and struggling to rise out of poverty, preserve historical buildings, and bring gay and lesbian issues to the public agenda. Many of the founders, who learned to use the gestetner and write a press release at MOVE, are still around today at places such

Johanna Oosterveld.

as the North End Community Health Centre and the Ecology Action Centre.

After a few years organizing bank workers for the Canadian Labour Congress, Oosterveld spent 10 years as director of the North End Community Health Centre. She clearly recognized social ills (pressures individuals undergo in society) as health issues, and the clinic's programs grew from the needs of those who used them. She also took a lead role in developing community health clinics across Nova Scotia.

Oosterveld chaired the regional board for Oxfam, and served on the national executive. Health concerns in Namibia inspired her, and Oxfam's Johanna Oosterveld Fund continues to support work in rural health clinics in southern Africa.

Halifax activist Muriel Duckworth said Johanna encouraged her for her unexpected TV news debut when Duckworth asked the 12 men on the Halifax Citizens' Summit: "Where are the women?"

Oosterveld's children remember their mother as the rock on which they built their lives. Her driving motivation made the world better for children, and she seemed to find balance between public and private. She believed strongly that each person contributes in a meaningful way to a civilized society, and when she talked, people understood.

A honeysuckle vine reaches across the fence in a back yard in Halifax's OVO Co-op where a brass plaque to Oosterveld is buried in its foliage: a memorial to a woman who helped change how we live in Halifax today.

— *Gwen Davies*

MATTHEW PENNELL, SR.
C. 1714-1801

For 45 years the Pennell family manned the Sambro Island Light with Matthew Pennell, Sr. taking on the job after his days as a privateer ended. Two of his sons, Matthew, Jr. and Henry, followed their father in the lonely enterprise.

In 1757, Captain Pennell, a native of the Channel Islands, near France, was fined for breaching privateering regulations, after his schooner *Musquito*, owned by Halifax merchant Joshua Mauger, took coffee, cocoa and sugar from the Dutch ship *Patience* in what was probably one of the first prizes of the Seven Years' War.

In 1771, before Matthew Pennell, Sr. became the Sambro lightkeeper, the supply vessel *Granby* hit the Sambro Ledges during a raging storm, killing the crew, three petty officers and 12 naval officers. This caused an indignant outcry in London, which affected Pennell and his progeny for the next half century.

In 1772, Matthew, Sr. became the keeper for the next 27 years, until he was 85. His son, Matthew, Jr., told the provincial treasurer about a wild storm that wreaked havoc on the lighthouse. Twelve panes of glass blew out of the lantern and many more were damaged. Sea water violently filled the west end of the store and damaged the end of the building, filling the well and the cellar and nearly carrying the house with it.

In 1799, Matthew, Sr. complained about Mrs. James Moody, the contractor who supplied the Sambro light. The old lightkeeper claimed she had not credited him with his last year's salary and said if his health allowed, he'd take his complaint to Lieutenant Governor Sir John Wentworth to see if he'd turn him off the lighthouse island. He noted that he was not ordered there to tend the light but to keep a "good light" after the *Granby* sloop was cast away. Mrs. Moody, whose late husband had previously supplied a poor light, wanted Matthew, Sr. removed.

After Matthew Pennell, Jr. took over, the Assembly granted his father

£100 a year. After Matthew, Sr. died in 1800, his wife Agnes petitioned the Assembly for money. She received £25.

Matthew, Jr. petitioned Lieutenant Governor John Sherbrooke in 1814 praying for a new dwelling as poor weather would make his current home uninhabitable. He also mentioned the salary, still £100, noting that providing provisions and wages for his two assistants nearly consumed his entire wage.

When Matthew, Jr. died in 1816 his brother, Henry, noted in the *Halifax Gazette* that all persons indebted to the Pennell estate should "make immediate payment to Henry Pennell." Henry took the £65 estate for himself claiming he had worked eight years at the Sambro Light, which he had not. He claimed the property plus the money owed to his father. His four married sisters in Ketch Harbour questioned Henry's integrity and accused him of embezzlement.

It appears that Henry Pennell was the last Pennell lightkeeper. In 1817, he received £50 from Samuel Cunard for five months of service.

The Pennell name has not entirely disappeared. On mariners' charts, Pennell Shoal is recorded off Outer Sambro Island. There, the unmanned lighthouse serves as a beacon of safety for all seafarers who navigate the mouth of Halifax Harbour.

— *Joe McDonald*

RICHARD PRESTON
C. 1790-1861
Buried at Crane Hill, East Preston

Richard Preston is considered one of the most important black leaders in Nova Scotia. He was born a slave but destined for greatness as a literate, captivating preacher from Virginia. Fleeing slavery and searching for his mother, Preston came north as a refugee of the War of 1812. When he arrived in Halifax, he heard she was living in Preston. The township so welcomed and shaped him that he took its name as his own.

Preston wasted no time getting involved in Nova Scotia's black community. John Burton, leader of the Halifax Baptists, helped Richard become the first black delegate to the Nova Scotia Baptist Association and encouraged him to become a minister. Baptist church deacons sent Preston to England for ordination, and to solicit much-needed funds to establish a new church.

In London, Preston met William Wilberforce, the noted abolitionist, and upon returning to Nova Scotia formed the African Abolition Society. Preston returned in 1832 as Father Preston, and his newly funded African

Having escaped slavery in the American South, Richard Preston was a dynamic leader, challenging racism in Halifax society during the 1830s.

Chapel attracted many disgruntled members of Burton's parish.

The African Chapel became the centre of the community for many black Nova Scotians. With wit and authority, Father Preston preached the virtues of God and of abolition "as fluid on the platform as in the pulpit," wrote P.E. MacKerrow in *A Brief History of the Coloured Baptists of Nova Scotia.*

Preston travelled the province on horseback and by carriage, founding 11 churches in communities including Hammond's Plains, Annapolis, Salmon River, Bear River, Digby and Weymouth. In 1854, he helped form the 12-church African Baptist Association of Nova Scotia, which fostered a black consciousness among African Nova Scotians. It has been said the association kept blacks from many mainstream opportunities. However, it must be kept in mind that back in those days blacks were barred from most public places.

Although slavery had ended in Nova Scotia, discrimination continued. In the 1830s, the Legislative Council refused Father Preston a grant for the African Chapel. The drive for responsible government in the 1840s could have provided Preston with a further area of activism. In the crucial 1847 election, however, he backed the losing Tories, worried that reforms might damage Nova Scotia's connections with Britain. The policies of the new reform government actually marginalized blacks, so Preston continued to promote his policy of separatism from mainstream white society.

Preston died in 1861, the first year of the American Civil War. The former slave, who dedicated his life to winning the freedom of others and spreading God's word, did not live to see the abolition of slavery in the country of his birth.

— *Jennifer Morrison*

WIELSAW ROBACZEWSKI (WESTON ROBERTS)
1925-2001
Buried at Oakridge Memorial Gardens, Lower Sackville

Wielsaw Robaczewski (Weston Roberts).

Weston Roberts quietly left his mark on many buildings that Nova Scotians will use for generations. For 35 years, his name appeared on Nova Scotia's construction records as the structural engineer for such buildings as the Public Archives, the Halifax-Dartmouth ferry terminals and the Dartmouth Sportsplex.

He was born Wieslaw Robaczewski in 1925 in Warsaw, Poland, to a prominent family. When World War II began, his family fled the city to escape German invaders, only to find Russians on the eastern side. His father was arrested and disappeared. Learning that they were next, his mother Aurelia took the children and fled back to German-occupied Warsaw. By 1941, 16-year-old Robaczewski was involved in the conspiracy that culminated in the heroic 1944 Warsaw Rising — the biggest operation organized and executed by a partisan organization in World War II. When the Rising was put down, the wounded Robaczewski was sent to a German Prisoner of War Camp. After the camp's liberation, he joined the British Army and saw duty in Italy.

In 1947, he returned to Warsaw. As a decorated officer in the Polish Home Army, he was considered bourgeois and an enemy of the state by the newly installed Communist regime. Despite this, he managed to graduate from the Warsaw Polytechnical University with a Masters in Engineering.

In 1961, he moved to Canada with his wife, Maria, and two children. With limited language skills and foreign credentials, he worked hard to gain recognition in his field. In 1967, he started his own firm, W. Roberts Engineering Limited, which designed and oversaw the construction of thousands of projects throughout the Atlantic Provinces including schools, hospitals, sports facilities and laboratories.

A construction foreman at a large project recalled later how he called Roberts at 4 a.m., confessing in panic that he had discovered an error in the concrete pour. He expected his company would have to re-do the job at tremendous expense and he would likely lose his job. Roberts appeared half an hour later, looked over the problem, took measurements and made notes. He spent many early hours redesigning the elements to maintain the structural requirements. He calmly steered the changes and the building was completed without disruption. The foreman kept his job, and Roberts, known for his integrity, had a life-time admirer.

During his last 15 years, Roberts faced Parkinson's disease and many other health challenges with the same dignity and stoicism that marked his life.

— Veronika Larsen

ELROY ROBSON
1898-1986
Cremated in Halifax

For nearly 50 years, Elroy Robson served the Canadian working class as a dedicated and respected leader, distinguishing himself as a labour pioneer and activist who stood steadfastly for an independent, democratic all-Canadian labour movement.

Born in Halifax, Robson, one of six children, married Eva Trefontaine and they had two children. In 1942, he became the national vice-president of the Canadian Brotherhood of Railway, Transport and General Workers Union (CBRT), a position he held for 22 years. He also served the Ontario Federation of Labour as its first elected president, headed the Toronto Labour Council for 10 years, and served as Ontario regional director of the Canadian Congress of Labour, one of the forerunners of the present-day Canadian Labour Congress.

Robson and the CBRT played a courageous role in the struggle to overcome the 100-year domination of the Canada's labour movement by American-based unions. In the struggle to represent Canadian seamen, Robson, the "chief architect" of the fight, and the CBRT were largely responsible for defeating the corrupt, gangster-ridden Seafarers' International Union (SIU) led by the notorious Hal Banks. The SIU, in collusion with the St. Laurent government and the CLC, destroyed the Canadian Seamen's Union. A CBC/NFB docudrama, *Canada's Sweetheart: The Saga of Hal Banks*, tells this story: Robson is shown standing up to Banks, described as a ruthless dictator who brutalized seamen. "If you can't protect workers, I bloody well will," he tells a government official in the film.

With the support of an Ontario-based shipping firm, the CBRT boycotted SIU ships, making this "the most unusual and important labour-management alliance in Canadian history," notes William Kaplan in *Everything That Floats*. He called Robson and the shipping management "men who refused to sacrifice principle to present expediency."

During a 1961 federal commission to investigate the disruption in shipping, Robson appeared as a witness. An SIU lawyer insisted on calling him Robeson, "presumably alluding to the well-known American communist opera and folk singer."

A representative on the Ontario Regional War Board, Robson promoted labour's role in the Second World War. For that work and his contributions to the Canadian labour movement, the Order of the British Empire in 1946 honoured him with membership. Robson, who lived until the age of 88, spent his life standing for social justice for all working Canadians.

— John St. Amand

MAJOR-GENERAL ROBERT ROSS
1766-1814
Buried at the Old Burying Grounds, Halifax

Although Major-General Robert Ross had a brilliant and heroic military career during the Napoleonic Wars, he is best remembered for his achievements during the War of 1812.

Ross was born in Rostrevor, Northern Ireland. After graduating from Trinity College in Dublin, he joined the British Army in 1785, rising to the rank of Major by 1799. With his own command in 1803, he saw action in Egypt, Italy, the Netherlands and Spain, and assisted the Duke of Wellington. Although he was a strict disciplinarian, his troops admired him and he won four Gold Medals, a Sword of Honour and public thanks from Britain's Parliament for his heroism and leadership. When war broke out with the United States in 1812 he was promoted to the rank of Major General.

He invaded Washington, D.C., on August 24, 1814 and entered the "President's House" shortly after President Madison's wife, Dolly, had fled, leaving a hot breakfast on the table. He was given the historic order to burn the mansion after it was plundered. The deep burn marks were covered with white paint during its restoration, and it was renamed the "White House."

Ross's fateful attack on Baltimore followed on September 12, but what he had assumed would be an easy win would instead prove his downfall. He was shot dead by two privates in the American volunteer militia.

The now-famous Frances Scott Key was a civilian prisoner aboard a British ship during Ross's attack on Fort McHenry near Baltimore. He was so inspired by the bombs exploding and the U.S. flag still flying through the mayhem that he wrote the "Star Spangled Banner." General Ross died a British hero, but one who inadvertently created two of America's greatest patriotic symbols: the White House and the U.S. national anthem.

Major-General Ross's body was preserved in a keg of rum for shipment to Nova Scotia and his final burial in Halifax's historic "Old Burial Grounds." It is said that as a mark of a hero, his faithful troops drank from his funeral keg. One irony of history is that as many Americans as Canadians and British visit Ross's tomb in Halifax. Another is the fact that his tomb lies directly across the street from North America's oldest consecutively occupied executive mansion, Government House.

— *Allan Doyle*

CALVIN RUCK
1925-2004
Buried at Dartmouth Memorial Gardens, Dartmouth

Canadian senator Calvin Ruck became a human rights activist after moving to Halifax and experiencing racism for the first time. Growing up in Whitney Pier, the son of Barbadian immigrants George and Ida Ruck, he lived happily among many ethnic groups.

Ruck left school after grade 10, worked as a labourer at the Dominion Steel and Coal Mill, and then in 1945 joined Canadian National Railways as a sleeping-car porter, the only job available to blacks. When other blacks complained to Ruck about their treatment, he said he felt uncertain about protesting for fear they would lose their jobs. But Ruck was "a soft-spoken social activist," who left the railway in 1958 and found his voice as an activist. "I felt obliged to protest," he told the *Sunday Daily News* in 1998. "We've been brainwashed to be passive."

In the fifties, barbers in Dartmouth refused to cut the hair of black customers until threatened with legal pressure. When Ruck and his wife, Joyce, bought land in 1954 and built a home in a Dartmouth suburb, the neighbours petitioned to keep them out because they were worried the Rucks would build a sub-standard home. Their petition was unsuccessful after he presented his house plans. He also had trouble getting an apartment, after inquiring in the store below the apartment building. He was told to ask all

In 1993, Calvin Ruck became Canada's third black senator.

the tenants if they approved of a black tenant. He refused. As an advocate he often quoted human rights laws when black citizens were refused apartments and jobs. "He was a guy who worked from the bottom up," Henry Bishop of the Black Cultural Centre told *The Globe and Mail*. "He was a peaceful warrior and a drum major for justice."

After working 10 years as a cleaner at Canadian Forces Base Shearwater, he became a social worker in Preston — his most rewarding work — and received a diploma in social work from Dalhousie University in 1979. He later served on the Nova Scotia Human Rights Commission for five years and volunteered in many community organizations. He wrote two books, *The Black Battalion 1916-1920: Canada's Best Kept Military Secret* and *Canada's Black Battalion: No 2 Construction, 1916-1920*, to promote neglected Black history and culture.

Calvin Ruck received many honours for his work, including two honorary degrees and the Order of Canada in 1995. He was one of three Canadians to receive a Harry Jerome award for community service. In 1993, he became the third black person appointed to the Senate. After Ruck's death in 2004, Burnley 'Rocky' Jones, a lawyer and activist, told the *Chronicle-Herald* that "[h]e was a hell of a man."

— *Roma Senn*

JOHN SAVAGE
(1932-2003)
&
MARGARET SAVAGE
(1932-2003)

Both cremated with ashes buried at Mount Hermon Cemetery, Dartmouth

John Savage was the front man, the family doctor, mayor and premier. Margaret was the backbone, the quiet counsel at the kitchen table, the woman who worked to feed the hungry and deliver books to those who couldn't get out of the house.

Together, John and Margaret made a powerful presence in Nova Scotia, penetrating the highest political echelons and at the same time touching people on the ground who needed their help.

Immigrants from the United Kingdom, John and Margaret settled in Dartmouth in the 1960s and brought up seven children.

John's first calling was medicine, but a passion for social reform led him into politics. After serving as mayor of Dartmouth, he was elected Liberal premier in a tumultuous tenure driven by a municipal amalgamation and an agenda to clean up the tradition of political patronage — a system he regarded as deeply unfair and bad for Nova Scotia. But he learned that old habits die hard and, in the end, the premier's drive to end the patronage cost him his job.

This political failure was not emblematic of his entire political career. John understood that politics is more than elections, legislatures and formal office. This was evident during his time as mayor when he convened a secret group of mayors, provincial cabinet ministers and senior bureaucrats to address social problems in Halifax, Dartmouth and the County.

The Saturday Morning Group worked behind the scenes pulling together community projects, which included residences for addicted homeless men, shelters and second-stage housing for people in crisis.

To both Savages, politics also meant getting out, rolling up your sleeves and getting dirt under your fingernails. This is exactly what happened when they worked with a committee of volunteers to disassemble the old United Church in Cole Harbour and rebuild it again in North Preston to give that community its first medical centre and day care.

There's no doubt that John's fingernails came back dirty after a journey to war-torn Nicaragua to provide medical aid and later to Niger where he set up a medical clinic.

While always a partner in these initiatives, Margaret championed her own causes. From her kitchen table, she promoted projects for global development and to feed the hungry in her own community. She was also a driving force behind the Dartmouth Book and Writing Awards.

John and Margaret died in 2003 within months of one another, but the fingerprints of the Savage political legacy will remain on Halifax Regional Municipality for a long time.

— Gail Lethbridge

JOSEPH SCOTT
1724-1800
Buried at All Saints Anglican Cemetery, Bedford

Without a doubt, Joseph Scott was the largest landowner ever in the Bedford area. In 1759, he received a land grant of 850 acres, and six years later, a second grant of 700 acres, followed by another 16 acres in 1776 next to Fort Sackville, where he built his home.

On his first 850 acres, he built the first sawmill in the area and later a grist mill. His second parcel of land assured there would be sufficient lumber for his mills and a steady supply of lumber for export to England. His brother, George, who was killed in a duel in 1767, left Nova Scotia lands to Scott. In 1759, Scott acquired another extensive land tract in Hants County, which extended from the Avon and St. Croix Rivers to St. Margaret's Bay. Scott established new settlements in this area and, to that end, brought over the

This painting of Joseph Scott's home by Anneke Betlam was donated to the Scott Manor House.

Dill and Smith families from Ireland. Descendants of the Dill family still live in the area and are noted for their giant pumpkins.

Scott was born in a large manor house in Balingary, Ireland, in 1714, the third of eight children in an Irish Protestant family. He died in his own Scott Manor in Sackville, now Bedford.

He came to Halifax when he was 25 and single, with the first group in Governor Edward Cornwallis's fleet in 1749, arriving on the ship *London*, and listed as a quartermaster in the 67th Foot Regiment under Governor Shirley of Massachusetts. The following year he married Mary Morris, believed to be the daughter of Charles, the chief surveyor of Nova Scotia and Halifax's first town planner. The couple had four children, but, unfortunately, Mary and the children died within a few years. In 1763, Scott married Margaret Ramsey Cottnam in Halifax.

Scott, a merchant, sold everything from London china to beaver coating, linens, cod lines, stockings, coffee pots, Irish butter, soap and rum. He built 10 Mile House, an inn that still stands in Bedford today; served as a justice of the peace and a judge of the inferior court of common pleas; was a surveyor of lumber; and was elected to the second House of Assembly in Nova Scotia.

Circa 1772, Scott and Margaret built their large manor house adjacent to Fort Sackville at the Head of the Bedford Bay. They lived there with their two children, Elizabeth and Michael, numerous servants and farm hands, and likely entertained people like Richard Uniacke and Prince Edward. Scott House remains as an historic reminder of his life.

— Ann MacVicar

IRA SETTLE
1908-1995
Buried at Woodlawn Cemetery, Dartmouth

Living through most of the twentieth century, Ira Settle saw tremendous changes in farming and every other aspect of life. He enjoyed life's journey and made the most of it as a farmer, councillor and warden.

As the youngest in his family, Settle was bright and observant as a child. When his mother died soon after his birth, his older sisters cared for him. He learned to farm and do an honest day's work from his father and brothers. He went everywhere with his father and developed a keen interest in people and the world around him, learning and storing memories to draw on later.

As a young man, he read newspapers avidly and followed local and world affairs with interest. He had a great ability to listen to his many

Ira Settle hoes lettuce in his Cole Harbour garden. Photo c.1990.

friends, neighbours and colleagues, weighing the relevant information and suggesting a practical course of action before others had finished discussing it.

A good student and keen on sports, especially baseball, Settle pulled on the lightweight tug-of-war team with other Cole Harbour farm boys. He finished his studies at the one-room Cole Harbour School and passed his provincial exams successfully. Further education was cut short when his father had an accident that required his son's help in running the farm. Settle never regretted the choice.

During his years as councillor and then warden of Halifax County, his days usually began and ended with several hours in his market garden. He worked his land well into his eighties. He produced top-quality produce and marketed it with entrepreneurial skill to Halifax grocery stores.

In addition to the many community improvements during his political career, Settle contributed to many more, generously donating his time, energy, talents, money and materials. Always modest, he enjoyed seeing the improvements from his efforts. To this day, Settle is still remembered by many for his friendly handshake that began and ended every encounter.

— *Elizabeth Corser*

SAMUEL LEONARD SHANNON

1816-1895

Buried at Camp Hill Cemetery, Halifax

A romantic who once serenaded a young girl by placing a wound music box in a watering can and hoisting it aloft on a garden rake below her window, Samuel Leonard Shannon met his wife, Annie Fellows, when she was a child of eight and he a 27-year-old solicitor. They married in 1855 when she turned 20. In the intervening years, Shannon made preparations for marriage, securing a three-story house on the corner of Spring Garden Road and Brenton Street, and a burial plot in Camp Hill Cemetery. The first of 10 children arrived when he was 41, the last when he was 63.

Raised in Halifax, one of Shannon's favourite recollections was of the winter of 1820-21 when Halifax Harbour froze and his father, James Noble Shannon, carried him on his shoulders across to Dartmouth. A lover of history and classics, he graduated from Halifax Grammar School and the University of King's College before turning to law. He was called to the Bar in 1839. Specializing in wills and real estate, Shannon opened an office on Bedford Row.

Shannon pursued his interest in things military and ceremonial by joining the Queen's Halifax Militia Regiment. He especially enjoyed riding his favourite steed, Agamemnon, in parades. While waiting for Annie to grow up, Shannon undertook a nine-month grand tour of Europe in 1848. A great conversationalist, humourist and storyteller, he dined out for years on tales of his encounters with the Chartist Riots, the Paris revolutionaries and the Battle of Sunderbund.

Shannon was highly respected locally. He successfully ran as a Conservative candidate in Nova Scotia in 1859 and 1863. His belief, however, that a Canadian Confederation would bring political and commercial advantages to Nova Scotians and keep them "from flooding to Boston", resulted in his defeat in 1867. Nonetheless, Queen Victoria bestowed on him the title "Honourable" for his support.

A church and community-oriented man, Shannon was a trustee of the YMCA and president of both the Nova Scotia Bible Society and the Nova Scotia Evangelical Alliance. In 1881, he was appointed a Judge of Probate. He was also instrumental in setting up Dalhousie Law School, where he taught on a part-time basis.

In spite of his age, Shannon was a man of foresight who believed that a very different world was coming: "we are on the threshold of still greater things for assuredly the world will yet be girdled by the electric wire."

— *Della Stanley*

JOHN SIMON
1876-1966
Buried at Baron De Hirsch Cemetery, Halifax

After buying the once-elegant Queen Hotel at a give-away price of $17,500 during the Depression, John Simon failed to follow the fire inspector's requirements, resulting in one of the worst fires in Halifax, killing 28 people and injuring 19.

The fire at the Queen Hotel on Hollis Street began early on March 2, 1939. The desk clerk, noticing billows of smoke, began phoning guests, as there was no fire alarm system. He made one call before heavy smoke forced him out of the building. The firefighters arrived quickly to a frantic scene. Though some of the guests managed to climb to the roof at the back of the hotel, the roof collapsed, killing them all. A father reluctantly dropped his two young children nine metres into a life net below before jumping to safety himself. A firefighter recalled seeing a woman surrounded by flames, praying. He couldn't save her. It was impossible for the firemen to reach many of the guests because of the trolley cables and overhead power lines outside, and their ladders couldn't even reach the top floor.

At about noon, when the fire subsided, the devastated street looked like it had been "ripped by a tornado," the *Halifax Herald* reported. The Nova Scotia Legislature adjourned that day out of respect for the dead and their families. Two inquiries were called immediately.

The government-held Royal Commission blamed hotel owner Simon, a businessman who also ran the Hochelaga Shipping and Towing Company. Simon failed to carry out the safety measures called for by the fire inspector. His employees were never instructed in fire procedure and there were no signs in the halls to show escape routes, nor ropes from the windows. The iron exterior fire-escape ladders were fitted with wooden landings that burned away quickly, and access to them ran through rooms that were generally locked.

At an inquiry, fire inspector Phillip Ring said he had made four recommendations but had never returned to ensure that they were carried out. The fire department also received criticism in another inquiry for its outdated equipment.

Simon was charged with criminal negligence but was found not guilty, as it could not be proven that proper safety features would have saved all the guests' lives. He was also sued by the survivors' families and later faced another criminal charge for breaching fire regulations in another group of buildings.

Simon died in 1966 at the age of 90 in a Halifax nursing home. His obituary makes no mention that he'd ever owned the Queen Hotel.

— *Roma Senn*

FLEMMING SMITH
C. 1815-1910
Believed to be buried at St. John's Cemetery in Sackville, though a grave marker has not been found

Although Flemming Smith was one of many Bedford entrepreneurs, his story is unique: he was the son of Virginia slaves who escaped during the War of 1812.

It is believed that his mother, a capable woman who learned nursing skills from her "master Doctor," escaped from the plantation by boat. According to Flemming, who wasn't born then, his mother threw a feather bed into a boat, put her children in and rowed out into Chesapeake Bay where Admiral William Wallis picked them up in a British man-of-war and brought them to Halifax. Her husband, who had fled earlier, was also rescued by the British. It is said that when Mrs. Smith arrived in Halifax, she was surprised and elated to see her husband standing on the docks.

Late in his life Flemming Smith contacted the admiral and recounted the story of his parents' rescue and arrival in Halifax. The admiral wrote back and enclosed a signed picture, which Flemming prized and proudly showed visitors.

Flemming was born circa 1815 in Nova Scotia and worked as a farmer, railway worker, singing teacher, clerk and waiter at the Bellevue and Fitzmaurice Hotels in Bedford. Known for his pleasant disposition and impeccable dress in black tails and white gloves, he was a flamboyant story-teller with an appreciation for life, and was quoted by Elsie Tolson in *The Captain, The Colonel and Me*: "He who has tasted a sour apple will have more relish for a sweet one."

During Flemming's life, Bedford was a working-class mill town with an early tourism trade in cottages, summer homes, hotels and inns — a destination for outings. In 1837, Flemming opened the Flemming Smith Picnic Grounds in the area between the Anglican graveyard and the Dartmouth Road. The park had swings and tilts for children, picnic tables and benches. Flemming and his wife made beer and candy for picnickers and entertained them with gospel singing and story telling.

People travelled from Halifax and Dartmouth to hear his marvellous stories. Many arrived by boat, docking at the foot of Wardour Street, a five-minute stroll to the grounds.

In his old age, Flemming moved from his small house on the picnic grounds to Cobequid Road. Descendents of this respected entrepreneur still live in the area.

— *Ann MacVicar*

TITUS SMITH
1768-1850
Buried at Titus Smith Park, Halifax

Titus was born in Granby, Massachusetts, in 1768, and came to Nova Scotia with his Loyalist parents in 1783. By the time he died in 1850, on his 47th wedding anniversary, he enjoyed the reputation of knowing a great deal about nearly everything.

Smith has been hailed as "a pioneer of plant ecology in this continent," and as the man with whom began "the systematic study of Nova Scotia's natural endowments." By trade he was a land surveyor and farmer, but he was much more than that. He wrote petitions, selected and planted the original trees surrounding Province House, entered and won agricultural competitions, served as a road overseer, and edited *The Colonial Farmer*. When Maria Morris painted the watercolours for her *Wildflowers of Nova Scotia*, Smith wrote the descriptive text. He traveled to Québec to testify to the Durham Commission, lectured at the Mechanics' Institute, and translated German stories. Somewhere in all of this, he and his wife raised 14 children.

In 1801, Governor Sir John Wentworth charged Smith to report on "the soil, the situation of the lands, and the species, quality and size of the tim-

Titus Smith was among Nova Scotia's pioneer naturalists.

bers." He did that and estimated acreages and discussed "the possibility and means of rendering them fit for cultivation." When Smith saw abuses of nature, he would suggest a remedy. He reported on wild animal stocks and denounced the destruction of moose and beaver and wildlife habitat. He made observations on the uses of flora, on mineral potential, and just about everything else.

Between May 1801 and October 1802, Smith made three lengthy trips through Nova Scotia's wilderness, spending 150 days in the woods, equipped only with what he could carry, a compass and a map, "which," he said, "was probably as much hindrance as help."

The "Dutch Village Philosopher" taught consistently for half a century that the land is rich with the bounty of a wise Providence. Through our intelligence, we humans can discover the means to assist the soil to yield in abundance. We must not destroy our natural environment through careless-ness or the desire of a few to profit.

For Titus Smith, the solution to meeting human needs was not through more industrialization, but by a more rational and intensive use of land and forest. He was truly a man for all seasons.

— *Terrence M. Punch*

JOHN SPROTT
1780-1869
Buried at Pioneer Cemetery, Middle Musquodoboit

When Musquodoboit Valley Presbyterians celebrated their centenary in 1915, the name Reverend John Sprott was already legendary.

John Sprott was born in 1780 in Stony Kirk, Wigtonshire, Scotland. He studied at the University of Edinburgh before immigrating to Nova Scotia in 1818, and preached in Windsor before accepting the call from Musquodoboit in 1825. Although he retired in 1849, he remained an active minister and lived on his farm in Middle Musquodoboit until his death in 1869.

Sprott ministered to the Presbyterians in the Musquodoboit Valley and also to their brethren along the Eastern Shore. He was a contributor to numerous Nova Scotian newspapers including *The Novascotian*, *Presbyterian Witness*, *Colonial Churchman* and *Morning Chronicle*, and to Scotland's *Galloway Advertiser* and *Stranraer Free Press*. His topics included Presbyterian Church activities, biographies of early Presbyterian clerics, and descriptions of the Musquodoboit Valley and Eastern Shore.

In 1825, there was only one Presbyterian Church and one log schoolhouse in the Musquodoboit Valley; before Sprott died, the river valley had seven churches and 14 schools.

Sprott had great concern for the spiritual welfare of his congregation. One family was moving to another province and passed by his gate at 4:00 a.m. The cleric was waiting for them at this early hour; he knelt on the road and prayed for their safe journey.

He was also eminently practical. On another occasion, the wet weather had finally abated; wheat was ready to be stored in the barn but there were more thunderclouds on the horizon. After Sprott ascended to his pulpit, he pointed to a member of the congregation and told him to go home at once and take in his wheat. Then he pointed at one or two others and instructed them to go and help.

Chief Justice John Sprott Archibald's article "Reminiscences and Reflections" in *Centenary of Presbyterianism in the Musquodoboit Valley* (1915) mentions that even after Sprott's death a number of people publicly laid such stress on Sprott's wit and humour that his great character as a Christian minister was almost eclipsed.

Other accounts all include anecdotal stories about this luminary. One mentions that Sprott disapproved of musical instruments during church service. However, a member of his congregation insisted on playing his kirk fiddle. One Sunday, Sprott could no longer endure the music of that instrument. Before the closing hymn he announced "[we] will fuddle and sing to the Glory of God in the 119th Psalm. Basil! Basil! Get my horse!" Sprott descended from the pulpit and walked calmly out of the church as the fiddle wailed forth the first of the 176 verses.

Although he retired in 1849, Sprott remained an active minister and lived on his farm in Middle Musquodoboit until his death in 1869. His son, Reverend George W. Sprott, edited his father's letters, newspaper stories and memoirs, which were published in *Memorials of the Rev. John Sprott* (Edinburgh, 1906).

— *Philip Hartling*

GEORG TINTNER
1917-1999
Cremated in Halifax

Anyone fortunate enough to have seen Georg Tintner conducting Symphony Nova Scotia could never doubt his consuming passion for music; his feet barely touched the stage as he rose and dipped to the strains of Beethoven and Mozart. His small frame exemplified a taut wire of energy as

Georg Tintner was the music director of Symphony Nova Scotia from 1987 to 1994.

he conducted his musicians. His white hair, thick and flying, added its own drama to the performance.

Tintner was born in Vienna in 1917 and, from a tender age, he knew that music would be his destiny. At six, he was studying piano and composing shortly thereafter. He sang in the renowned Vienna Boys Choir and at 16, his compositions were broadcast. By the age of 19, he was assistant conductor at the Vienna Volksoper.

Fleeing the Nazi occupation in 1938, he made his way to New Zealand and Australia where, over the next several years, he appeared with every orchestra and opera company in those countries. He also held conducting positions in South Africa and with Sadler's Wells in London.

By the time Tintner was named music director of Symphony Nova Scotia in 1987, he had already been engaged eight times to conduct and mentor the National Youth Orchestra of Canada. He was an untiring musician, a perfectionist who took the Symphony to a totally new level. Cellist Shimon Walt explains: "He was thorough and methodical in his approach; he brought his particular brand of magic to music and the whole orchestra followed."

A consummate musician, Tintner was in great demand across Canada and made guest appearances with all of the major symphonies. In 1994, he was named Symphony Nova Scotia's Conductor Laureate, a position he held until his death in 1999.

He conducted operas throughout the world and also recorded extensively. He received two Doctor of Laws degrees: one from Dalhousie University in 1989, and the other from St. Francis Xavier University in 1995. The Province of Nova Scotia honoured him with the Portia White Prize, and the Government of Canada awarded him with both the Commemorative Medal for the 125th Anniversary of Canadian Confederation and the Order of Canada in 1998.

A vegetarian and pacifist, Tintner believed in protecting the environment and walked or bicycled everywhere. Following one performance, he was delighted when the Symphony presented him with a new 10-speed bicycle for his birthday.

— Pam Lutz

DEVENDRA PRASAD VARMA
1923-1994
Cremated in Halifax

Devendra Varma, an internationally acclaimed scholar, resurrected eighteenth- and nineteenth-century tales of ghosts, ghouls and vampires. An English professor at Dalhousie University, Dr. Varma loved stories of terror and horror, from Frankenstein to Prince Dracula, and his life's work made him a world-renowned authority on romantic Gothic literature.

Dr. Varma was born in 1923 in Darbhanga, India. He taught in Kathmandu, Syria and Cairo until 1963 when Dalhousie President Henry Hicks invited him to teach in the university's English department. One of his students called him "one of the most memorable professors [he] ever had."

Throughout his career, Dr. Varma researched lost or forgotten Gothic novels, traveling the world to find scarce original copies. These novels flourished in their own time as popular entertainment, but Dr. Varma rewrote, edited and republished more than 200 of those works. Some of his most famous include *The Gothic Flame* (1987), and *Voices from the Vaults: Authentic Tales of Vampires and Ghosts* (1988).

Dr. Varma, who has been described as a "genuine Renaissance man," traveled the world to seek the truth behind Gothic folklore, visiting the home of Frankenstein and delving deep into haunted woods in Germany. His greatest interest, however, was investigating true modern-day accounts of vampires all over North America and Europe. He called Bram Stoker's *Dracula* "probably the greatest horror tale of modern times." The

Hollywood Count Dracula Society recognized Dr. Varma for his achievements in the study of the dark prince.

In 1973, he visited Count Dracula's castle in Transylvania, in modern-day Romania. With a flair for the dramatic arts, Dr. Varma told his chilling story to Queen's University students on Halloween eve in 1986. According to the *Kingston Whig-Standard*, Dr. Varma said that as he explored the castle, the eerie silence was broken only by the sounds of footsteps quickly approaching and then moving away. "The shades of evil pervade this place even today like an icy breath from the past," he told the *Chronicle-Herald*.

The Government of Slovenia knighted Dr. Varma for his work on Gothic literature, which stands as a great achievement and inspired others in the field. Before he died, the University of Northern Colorado set up a Gothic literary society in his honour. The "Varma Goths" continue to meet to discuss the gripping tales that Dr. Varma loved.

— Ainslie MacLellan

ANGELA VECCHIO-OZMON
1964-2004
Cremated in Halifax

Angela Vecchio-Ozmon, a single mother and cancer activist, refused to be a victim, and she challenged anyone who acted like one. Angela made her personal confrontation with breast cancer public through CBC's television programme *Health Matters*. For more than two years she invited Canada to look over her shoulder during a weekly series.

She was born in New Jersey in 1964. Her father was a United States Air force pilot who died in an accident before her birth. When her mother remarried, Angela moved first to Prince Edward Island and then to Halifax. In college, she studied psychology and public relations and then worked in development and fundraising. In 1999, when her children were in preschool, she discovered a lump in her breast during a self-examination. She had a mastectomy.

Two years later, she was diagnosed with terminal breast cancer. She turned the tables on bad news and made breast cancer activism her mission. "There's no point in living if you don't make it count," she said in an interview. Determined to educate young women about breast health, she invited the CBC to film every aspect of her experience. And as a spokesperson for the Canadian Breast Cancer Foundation, Angela delivered her message in a speaking tour throughout the Maritimes.

Her willingness to expose herself was welcome but disturbing. She divulged the details people really wanted to hear, such as how breast cancer affected her social life: "On the first date, I tell the guy I have two kids and cancer. If he sticks around for a second drink, he might be worth getting to know," she said.

Cameras followed Angela from the time she found out her cancer was terminal to her kitchen table as she helped her children with homework and tried to figure out what to tell them. "Lying is a waste of time — my time, their time, and our time together," she said.

She encouraged people to meet experience head on, whether in joy or in sorrow. Thousands of television viewers responded to her message, following her progress and communicating through her website. She inspired her viewers with her blunt honesty and appetite for living. "If this can happen to me, it can happen to you."

— *Meg Federico*

BILLY WELLS
1881-1971
Buried at Mount Olivet Cemetery, Halifax

William "Billy" Wells was the sole survivor of the Patricia's *crew following the Halifax Explosion. Photo c.1930.*

In 1899, 18-year-old Billy Wells considered what to do with his life and joined the Halifax Fire Department as a call fireman. As any rookie, the old guys more than likely gave him all the dirty jobs — cleaning the horse stalls, shovelling coal and cleaning the washrooms. But Wells worked his way up to steamer engineer, drove the horse-pulled steamer and operated it at fires.

When Halifax purchased the first motorized pumping engine in Canada, a 1913 LaFrance pumper, later named *Patricia*, Wells became a motor driver, a coveted position that paid him about $17.00 a week. Wells' brother Claude, also a fireman, drove Fire Chief Condon in the 1911 McLaughlin Buick. It was common practice for the brothers to race each other to fires. After all, they drove the department's only motorized vehicles.

On the morning of December 6, 1917, Wells and the rest of the crew at the West Street Station received a call for a fire at Pier 6. Thinking it was just another one of the many pier fires caused by the ships' hot coals being dumped onto the wooden wharf, what they found was a burning *Mont Blanc* drifting into the pier. The chief and deputy arrived, and after a quick size-up, they decided to fight the fire on the pier. Hose wagon No. 4 arrived along with other horse-drawn apparatus.

Then an explosion hit. The Halifax Explosion was classed as the largest non-nuclear blast in the world. In the aftermath, the chief, deputy chief, two captains and five hose-men died. Wells was at the wheel of the *Patricia* at ground zero and miraculously survived. Severely injured and wandering aimlessly with nothing but his pants, he was picked up by a unit protection wagon and taken to Camp Hill Hospital.

Wells eventually returned to work. He retired in 1926 at the age of 45. When he died in 1971, he still possessed half of the steering wheel from the *Patricia*. He received it as a keepsake for all that he had endured.

— Don Snider

JOHN WENTWORTH
1737-1820
&
FRANCES WENTWORTH
D. 1813
Buried in the crypt of St. Paul's Church

In eighteenth-century colonial New Hampshire, the Wentworths were the most prominent family in every regard.

John Wentworth was born into the Wentworth family on August 9, 1737. After he graduated from Harvard, John's father sent him to London to further the family's political and commercial interests. Through the Marquis of Rockingham's influence, John succeeded his uncle, Benning Wentworth, as New Hampshire's governor in 1766. When the American rebellion broke out in 1776, he did everything in his power to keep New Hampshire loyal to the Crown. But in that same year, he fled the colony with his wife Frances and their newborn son. Wentworth remained in London for the duration of the war and was able to secure the Office of Surveyor General of the King's Woods for the remaining North American colonies.

The Wentworths arrived in Halifax in September of 1783. For the next nine years, John traveled through the forests of Nova Scotia and New Brunswick marking the white pine forests with the King's Arrow to preserve them for mast timber. While away on his journeys, Frances is reputed to have had an affair with Prince William Henry, third son of George III.

John and Frances were fortuitously in England in December of 1791 when word was received of Governor John Parr's death. John was successful in obtaining the governorship and became Nova Scotia's first civilian governor.

The 1790s were the high tide of his governorship. War with Revolutionary France brought prosperity, as well as Prince Edward, fourth son of George III and Commander-in-Chief, to Nova Scotia.

The Wentworths entertained lavishly, especially after Frances became

Lady Frances Wentworth occupied a place of prominence within Halifax society throughout the later part of the eighteenth century. She is pictured here in 1765 at age 20.

Lady Wentworth on her husband receiving a baronetcy in 1795. An anonymous poet reflected John's popularity in verse on seeing his excellency Sir John Wentworth passing through Granville.

> But when our loyal WENTWORTH deigns to ride,
> (The Sovereign's fav'rite and the Subject's Pride,)
> Around his Chariot crowding Numbers throng,
> And hail his Virtues as he moves along.

However, from 1796, John's troubles mounted. His mishandling of the Jamaican Maroons — Africans who refused to live in slavery — nearly lost him the governorship. He was heavily in debt and increasingly unwell from 1803 onwards. He faced growing opposition in the Assembly over road appropriations, though he did manage to convince the members to vote funds for the Humane Establishment on Sable Island and the province's much admired and cherished Government House, a design that came from George Richardson's *A Series of Designs for County Seats*. As war with United States seemed ever more likely, the Government replaced the aging John Wentworth in 1808 with military officer Sir George Prevost.

In 1809, the Wentworths left for England where John hoped to settle his financial affairs. After a painful illness, Frances died in the arms of her son in 1813. Meanwhile, John had returned to Nova Scotia where he later died.

— *Brian Cuthbertson*

BENJAMIN WIER
1805-1868
Buried at the Camp Hill Cemetery, Halifax

The scandalous business ethics of one of Halifax's most controversial and successful economic visionaries, Benjamin Wier, not only riled the American White House. They also inadvertently helped push Nova Scotia into Confederation.

Wier was an inventive businessman. He became wealthy by 1845 — after several bankruptcies — with his Halifax shipping company. His wild Irish personality and political ideas soon attracted the political support of Joseph Howe.

Wier was first elected to Halifax Council in 1851 as a reformer and a liberal, and then elected to the Nova Scotia Legislature. Like Howe, he campaigned for a railway to connect Halifax's thriving industries with markets in Québec and Ontario, and he was soon on the boards of numerous businesses, from railways to banks. His boisterous public speaking in support of free trade with the United States was renowned.

In 1864, during the American Civil War, Wier hosted lavish balls in his Halifax mansion for many Southern "Blockade Runners," including the nephew of President Jefferson Davis and Captain James Taylor Wood. President Lincoln's Cabinet was outraged by Wier and Halifax's wildly profitable support for the South. The city seemed to host more Southerners than Atlanta. As a result, Wier was banned from the United States.

Meanwhile, a barrage of accusations that Wier was making a fortune at insider-profiteering during Nova Scotia's gold rush of 1863 facilitated the fall of the Joseph Howe government in 1864. Unfortunately for Wier, this helped his most ardent political enemy, pro-Confederation supporter Sir Charles Tupper, assume power and support John A. MacDonald. Howe and Wier would have negotiated a much different partnership.

Wier's banishment from the United States converted him to Tupper's Confederationist views, and with great vision he tried to convince Nova Scotia's wealthy industrial elite to readapt to having their markets in a united Canada. He was unsuccessful, and Canada's economic growth and protectionist tariffs would soon destroy Nova Scotia's powerful industrial base.

Nevertheless, a grateful MacDonald and Tupper made Wier a Canadian Senator in 1867 for all his efforts. He died a year later in Ottawa, and is remembered as one of the most intriguing politicians in Canadian history.
— *Allan Doyle*

CAPTAIN JOHN TAYLOR WOOD
D. 1904
Buried in Camp Hill Cemetery, Halifax

In the summer of 1864, the American Civil War came to Halifax when Captain John Taylor Wood and the Confederate cruiser *Tallahassee* sailed into Halifax Harbour for coaling and repairs. Wood could only remain in the neutral port for 24 hours, hardly enough time to complete his tasks. Added to his difficulties were two Union warships off Chebucto Head, waiting to pounce on him once he left. The city was buzzing with excitement.

In early August, the *Tallahassee*, a twin-screw, 61-metre, 500-ton iron steamer had slipped out of Wilmington to destroy Yankee shipping. Wood and his 120-man crew cruised north to Maine, burning or scuttling 26 vessels — a remarkable record. After two weeks, they desperately needed to refuel and repair a broken main mast. Accordingly, Wood sailed to Halifax, arriving on August 18.

As Wood's mast was not replaced in time, he received a 24-hour extension and requested a good pilot to guide him out of the harbour. In response, experienced Ketch Harbour pilot, Jock Fleming, came onboard. Fleming was described by Wood as a man of "Herculean proportions, bronzed by exposure to 60 seasons of storm and sunshine, who knew the harbour as well as the fish that swam its waters."

Wood asked if they could use Eastern Passage to avoid the Union cruisers outside the main channel. Fleming replied the water might be 4 metres deep, but he would not recommend taking the narrow and crooked channel. Wood assured Fleming if the water were that deep, he could keep his ship in the channel using her twin screws. Fleming accepted the challenge.

The vessel slipped her moorings that night, heading for Eastern Passage. In a remarkable feat of seamanship, Fleming kept the ship in the channel — considered impassable to all but small fishing boats — while Wood used one screw, then another, to twist and turn through the narrow passage. By midnight, the *Tallahassee* had come through, eluding the waiting Union cruisers.

When the war ended, Wood returned to Halifax and ran a shipping business until his death in 1904. Ironically, when he died he was secretary and treasurer of the Board of Pilot Commissioners.

For many years, the story of the *Tallahassee*'s escape was a favourite among the residents of Eastern Passage and was taught in the provincial school system. Today, the cruiser's presence remains in several Eastern Passage names.

— *John Boileau*

GEORGE HENRY WRIGHT
1849-1912
Buried at the monument in the family plot at Christ Church Cemetery, Dartmouth

One of the more intriguing characters in the history of the Halifax Regional Municipality is George Henry Wright, who was born in Dartmouth in 1849. The son of George and Bridget Murphy Wright, he was educated in Dartmouth and destined for the mercantile trade.

At the age of 17, his wanderlust got the best of him and he traveled to the United States, a common destiny for Maritime boys in the nineteenth century. Sometime in 1876 he began his life's work of compilation, which was at first a sort of "Bradshaw" (George Bradshaw produced the first travel guides) or "shippers guide" to industries. This work had him travel the length and breadth of America.

He traveled for four years before returning to New York. The outcome was *Wright's Australia, India, China, Japan Commercial Directory and Gazetteer.* It was first published in 1880, and distributed around the world by travel agents Thomas Cook & Sons. The publication would be enlarged and expanded over the years, and when the fifth edition was published in 1899, it was titled *The Australia, India, China, Japan Directory and Gazetteer embracing Canada, South and Central America, the West Indies and Africa.*

For many years, Wright lived in either New York City or London, England. In 1896, he returned to Halifax, where he became an active real estate developer, pamphleteer, sportsman and philanthropist. He became an active member of the Downtown Business Association. As a property developer, he built the Saint Paul Building and Wright Marble Buildings on Barrington Street and a mixed-income residential subdivision at the corner of South Park and Morris streets, including Wright Avenue and Wright Court. He also had houses built on Kent and Edward Streets.

Beginning in 1906, he began writing letters to newspapers on various topics, including profane language, immorality on screen and stage, indecent

Portrait of George Wright by the Halifax Notman Studio.

The Wright residence, 989 Young Avenue, Halifax.

literature and post cards, vandalism, better housing for the poor, and gambling. As a philanthropist, Wright gave generously to many causes.

With his return to Halifax, he became an active member of the Royal Nova Scotia Yacht Squadron. Between 1896 and 1912 he owned two yachts, the *Alba* and the *Princess*, and won outright the Plant, Colville-Gillett and Hesslein sailing cups. He also won the most prestigious of the squadron cups — the Prince of Wales — on three occasions. In June 1898, he donated the ebony-based, foot-tall, shaped, solid silver Wright Cup to the squadron.

He was an avid fisherman, who also shot. Interestingly, the newspapers are filled with references to his fish catches, but never a mention of his bagging any game. He played tennis with enthusiasm and was a member of the South End Tennis Club. In the 1890s, he also took up photography.

Wright usually traveled in the winter, returning to Halifax in the spring. That is how he came to book passage on the SS *Titanic* while in Paris. One of his traveling companions, C. W. Frazee, opined that Wright was such a heavy sleeper that he most likely slept through the sinking of the ship. Haligonian Hilda Slayter Lacon, in her recollections of the disaster, does not mention seeing Wright on deck, adding credence to Frazee's opinion.

In death, Wright was as generous as in life, leaving his splendid home on the corner of Young Avenue and Inglis Street to the Council of Women of Halifax and leaving more than $66,000 to charity. As a bachelor, the remainder of his estate was divided among his siblings and other relations. His brother James erected a simple monument: "Brother In Loving Memory of George Wright Lost on SS *Titanic* April 14, 1912. For If We Be Dead With Him, We Shall Also Live With Him."

— *Garry D. Shutlak*

CONTRIBUTORS

Patricia Arab, Edward Arab's first cousin, writes for *The Consulate*, a publication issued by the Office of the Consul of Lebanon.

Bruce Armstrong graduated in engineering from DalTech in 1969. He spent many years in England before returning to Nova Scotia and running into Pat Doherty.

Bridget Arsenault is a student at Mount Allison University where she writes for the *Argosy*, hosts a weekly radio program and contributes to CBC Moncton.

Chris Arsenault is a writer, broadcaster and social activist based in Halifax and is currently working on a book about the Zapatista rebellion.

Greg Arsenault is a graduate of Dalhousie Law School. He has practiced law in Halifax for the past 25 years.

Robert Ashe is an award-winning journalist and author of three books, including one on boxing in Halifax.

John Boileau began writing historical articles after retiring from the Canadian army. He was consulting editor for a history of the Canadian Forces and is the author of three non-fiction books.

Cyril Byrne is a member of the faculty of Saint Mary's University where he founded the D'Arcy McGee Chair of Irish Studies.

Sarah Cassidy graduated from the Convent of the Sacred Heart in 1976 and from Saint Mary's University in 1979. She has two daughters who are also Sacred Heart alumni.

Don Chard teaches Canadian history at Saint Mary's University and Mount Saint Vincent University. He has worked for Parks Canada and was a member of the Nova Scotia Legislature in 1998-99.

Sanjeev Chowdhury joined the Canadian Foreign Service in 1995 and has served overseas, as well as in Ottawa. In 2003, he was named Consul General of Canada to Ho Chi Minh City.

Marion Christie is a former newspaper reporter and high school teacher who is passionate about preserving the history of Bedford.

Elizabeth Corser has been with the Cole Harbour Rural Heritage Society since 1973 and has been the director of the Cole Harbour Heritage Farm Museum since 1988.

Stephen Coutts is the curator of the Nova Scotia Sports Hall of Fame in Halifax.

Brian Cuthbertson has written extensively on Nova Scotian history, including biographies of Richard John Uniacke, Sir John Wentworth and Bishop Charles Inglis.

Gwen Davies is a writer, teacher and plain language consultant and the founder of the Community of Writers retreat.

Peter Delefes is a retired school principal, a former MLA (Halifax-Citadel) and current president of the Heritage Trust of Nova Scotia.

Allan M. Doyle is a former history teacher with a passion for Nova Scotia. He promotes the need for regulation to preserve all heritage architecture in the province.

Graeme F. Duffus is an architect specializing in conservation. He is presently vice-president of the Heritage Trust of Nova Scotia and sits on the boards of Sacred Heart School of Halifax and the Fort Sackville Foundation.

A. E. (Tony) Edwards is a third-generation resident of Bedford. He is chair of the Bedford Heritage Society and a director of the Fort Sackville Foundation.

Meg Federico is a writer living in Halifax.

Marianne Ferguson came to Canada in 1939 with her family from what was then the Free State of Danzig, now Gdansk, Poland. In the late 1940s, she greeted immigrants and refugees at Pier 21, where she continues to volunteer today.

Judith Fingard has written widely on Canadian social history and the history of Halifax. She is co-editor with Janet Guildford of *Mothers of the Municipality: Women, Work and Social Policy in Post-1945 Halifax* and is currently president of the Royal Nova Scotia Historical Society.

Harry Flemming is a Halifax journalist whose work has been published in several Canadian newspapers and magazines.

Marie A. Gillen, SC, is director of heritage with the Sisters of Charity, Halifax. She holds a Masters of Arts degree in History and a doctorate in Educational Theory.

Frances Gregor discovered Clara MacIntosh's wide-ranging contributions to the city while researching the history of the Nova Scotia Council of St. John Ambulance.

Janet Guildford is a Halifax historian. She is co-editor with Judith Fingard of *Mothers of the Municipality*.

Carol Hansen attended NSCAD University (BA Fine Arts) and now divides her time between family, making art and restoring crumbling estates.

Justine Hart is a student and ski instructor who loves to sail in the summer.

Philip Hartling has a keen interest in built heritage. A reference archivist at Nova Scotia Archives and Records Management, he lovingly restored his great-grandparents' house in Port Dufferin.

Margaret Holgate is a work/life consultant who was introduced to the viol by Priscilla Evans in 1997 and now cannot imagine life without it.

Les Holloway was employed at the Halifax Shipyard and now works at the Marine Workers' Federation.

Sharon Ingalls is a founding member of the Rockingham Heritage Society and writes about local history for *Parkview News*.

C. Nelson Kennedy, a native of Bedford, has had a lifelong interest in Bedford's history and institutions. He is a director of the Fort Sackville Foundation.

Hannah Kovacs has lived in Halifax all her life. She is a second-generation Canadian and was thrilled to learn about her grandparents' past.

Sophie Langille-Broderick is a student from Dartmouth, N.S., who has learned more than she ever imagined possible by writing about her grandmother for this book.

John G. Langley, Q.C., is founding director and chairman of the Cunard Steamship Society. He is a passionate Nova Scotian with an abiding interest in maritime history, especially Cunard.

Veronika Larson's love of history and politics stems from attempting to understand how significant events in world history, such as the Second World War, came to occur.

Gail Lethbridge, a freelance writer living in Halifax, writes a weekly column for the *Chronicle-Herald* called Slacker Mom.

Jim Lotz has published 23 books, including *Green Horizons: Forests and Foresters in Nova Scotia* (Pottersfield Press) and *The Humble Giant: The Life and Times of Father M. Coady* (Novallis).

Pam Lutz enjoys a varied career in public relations and marketing, as well as an active involvement in musical theatre.

Mary Lynch, **MD**, **FRCPC**, is an associate professor of psychiatry at Dalhousie University and director of research at the Pain Management Unit at the Queen Elizabeth II Health Sciences Centre.

Ainslie MacLellan is a journalism student at the University of King's College in Halifax and has done broadcast news for CKDU FM.

Ann MacVicar has been recognized for her volunteer efforts in sports, recreation, church and heritage in Bedford and is currently chair of the Fort Sackville Foundation.

Allan Marble has written widely on medicine, science and genealogy. He is presently working on a history of medicine in Nova Scotia.

Joseph McDonald is a retired teacher from the Halifax area.

Mary Mohammed has lived in Halifax, Winnipeg and Vancouver. She owns and operates Mary's Bread Basket, which is famous for its cinnamon buns.

Jennifer Morrison is a student from Cole Harbour, N.S., and a former news editor with the *Dalhousie Gazette*.

Richard Norman is a graduate of the University of King's College. He currently lives in Brussels.

Mora Dianne O'Neill is associate curator, historical prints and drawings, for the Art Gallery of Nova Scotia and author of two books on Nova Scotia artists.

Lindsay O'Reilly is a writer and photographer with the *Reporter* in Port Hawkesbury, N.S.

Daniel N. Paul was born on the Indian Brook Reserve. He is an author, human rights activist, Justice of the Peace and board member for the provincial police commission.

Terrence M. Punch is resident genealogist for CBC Maritimes, and a columnist in *Saltscapes* and *Seniors' Advocate*.

Roxanne Rees was one of the first women to graduate from Royal Military College and now runs a multi-national company.

Bernard Riordon was the director of the Art Gallery of Nova Scotia before moving to the Beaverbrook Art Gallery in Fredericton, N.B.

Leah Kovacs Schweitzer, an Ottawa native, frequently visits her uncle and his family in Halifax.

Roma Senn has lived in Halifax for more than 25 years. She has a journalism degree from Carleton University and has worked for several newspapers and magazines.

Garry D. Shutlak has worked at Nova Scotia Archives and Records and Management since 1970 and has been active in heritage and historical topics for many years.

Carrie-Ann Smith is a writer and the manager of research at Pier 21, Canada's immigration museum.

Don Snider joined the Halifax Fire Department in May 1962. During his career, he became interested in the history of the Halifax Fire Service.

John St. Amand has worked as a union organizer for independent Canadian unions for more than 30 years and currently lectures in sociology at Dalhousie University.

Della Stanley is the coordinator of Canadian Studies and acting chair of Political and Canadian Studies at Mount Saint Vincent University.

Geraldine Thomas is a member of the faculty at Saint Mary's University where she teaches Classics. She is author of a book on the Greek community in the Maritime provinces.

Hazel Walling is a student at Dalhousie University.

Gus Wedderburn was born in Kingston, Jamaica, and came to Canada in 1952. He is past president of the NSACP, and a founding member of the Black United Front and the Black Education Centre. He helped build the Black Cultural Centre in Dartmouth, N.S.

Alfreda Withrow received a BA in History from Saint Mary's University and has been a historical researcher for various companies and government departments.

Lois Yorke has 25 years' experience as an archivist, editor, researcher, writer and consultant in cultural heritage, and is especially interested in the lives of Nova Scotian women.

SUGGESTED READING

Bell, John, ed. *Halifax: A Literary Portrait*. East Lawrencetown: Pottersfield Press, 1990.

Bruce, Harry. *An Illustrated History of Nova Scotia*. Halifax: Nimbus Publishing and the Province of Nova Scotia, 1997.

Chapman, Harry. *Along the Cole Harbour Road: A Journey Through 1765-2003*. Cole Harbour: Cole Harbour Rural Heritage Society, 2003.

Cuthbertson, Brian. *The Halifax Citadel*. Halifax: Formac Publishing, 2001.

Dogra, Ravi. *Indo-Canadians*. Tantallon: Four East Publications, 1987.

Fingard, Judith. *The Dark Side of Life in Victorian Halifax*. East Lawrencetown: Pottersfield Press, 1989.

Fingard, Judith; Guildford, Janet; and Sutherland, David. *Halifax: The First 250 Years*. Halifax: Formac Publishing, 1999.

Hartling, Philip L. *Where Broad Atlantic Surges Roll*. Halifax: Formac Publishing, 1979.

Jobb, Dean. *Bluenose Justice: True Tales of Mischief, Mayhem and Murder*. Hantsport: Lancelot Press, 1993.

Kimber, Stephen. *Sailors, Slackers and Blind Pigs: Halifax at War*. Toronto: Doubleday Canada, 2002.

LeBlanc, J.P., and Duivenvoorden, Trudy. *Pier 21: The Gateway that Changed Canada*. Hantsport: Lancelot Press, 1995.

Lotz, Pat. *Banker, Builder, Blockade Runner*. Kentville: Gaspereau Press, 2002.

MacKenzie, Shelagh, and Robson, Scott, ed. *Halifax Street Names: An Illustrated Guide*. Halifax: Formac Publishing, 2002.

Marshall, Dianne. *Georges Island: The Keep of Halifax Harbour*. Halifax: Nimbus Publishing, 2002.

Nova Scotia Archives and Records Management, "Halifax and Its People," Province of Nova Scotia, http://www.gov.ns.ca/nsarm/virtual/halifax

O'Neill, Mora Dianne. *The Artists' Halifax: Portraits of the Town and Harbour Through 250 Years*. Halifax: Formac Publishing, 2003.

Parker, Mike. *The Smoke-Eaters: A History of Firefighting in Nova Scotia c. 1750-1950*. Halifax: Nimbus Publishing, 2002.

Raddall, Thomas H. *Halifax: Warden of the North*. Halifax: Nimbus Publishing, 1993.

Thomas, Geraldine T. *Peoples of the Maritimes: Greeks*. Tantallon: Four East Publications, 2000.

Tolson, Elsie Churchill. *The Captain, The Colonel and Me: Bedford, Nova Scotia, Since 1503*. Bedford: The Tribune Press, 1979.

Watts, Heather, and Raymond, Michèle. *Halifax's Northwest Arm: An Illustrated History*. Halifax: Formac Publishing, 2003.

INDEX